Sharon Swain has done a multitude of jobs from
parish priest to team rector, and from rural dean to diocesan
adviser. She has written over a dozen books, including the
highly popular *Sermon Slot*, and taught on many diocesan adult
training courses. She is married with two children and, at present,
lives and works in Cumbria.

CONFIRMATION BOOK
FOR ADULTS

Sharon Swain

First published in Great Britain in 2008

Society for Promoting Christian Knowledge
36 Causton Street
London SW1P 4ST

Copyright © Sharon Swain 2008

All rights reserved. No part of this book may be reproduced or
transmitted in any form or by any means, electronic or mechanical,
including photocopying, recording, or by any information storage and
retrieval system, without permission in writing from the publisher.

SPCK does not necessarily endorse the individual views contained in its publications.

The author and publisher have made every effort to ensure that the
external website and email addresses included in this book are correct and
up to date at the time of going to press. The author and publisher are not
responsible for the content, quality or continuing accessibility of the sites.

Unless otherwise indicated, Scripture quotations are taken from the
New Revised Standard Version of the Bible, copyright © 1989 by the
Division of Christian Education of the National Council of the Churches
of Christ in the USA. Used by permission. All rights reserved.
Scripture quotations marked NIV are taken from the HOLY BIBLE,
NEW INTERNATIONAL VERSION, copyright © 1973, 1978, 1984
by International Bible Society. Used by permission of Hodder &
Stoughton Ltd, a member of the Hodder Headline Plc Group.

Common Worship: Services and Prayers for the Church of England is copyright
© The Archbishops' Council, 2000 and extracts are reproduced by permission.

The publisher and author acknowledge with thanks permission to
reproduce extracts from the following:
David Adam, Tides and Seasons, London: Triangle/SPCK, 1989, p. 20.

Every effort has been made to seek permission to use copyright material
reproduced in this book. The publisher apologizes for those cases
where permission might not have been sought and, if notified,
will formally seek permission at the earliest opportunity.

British Library Cataloguing-in-Publication Data
A catalogue record for this book is available from the British Library

ISBN 978–0–281–05955–3

1 3 5 7 9 10 8 6 4 2

Typeset by Graphicraft Ltd, Hong Kong
Printed in Great Britain by Ashford Colour Press

Produced on paper from sustainable forests

*This book is dedicated to the Revd Peter Streatfield,
with thanks for his work in the parishes*

Contents

Introduction

The *Confirmation Book for Adults* is intended to be a handbook for all adults who are either considering Confirmation or who are members of a Confirmation group. It can also be used to help those who are seeking to learn more about their faith, either as individuals or within a group, but who may already be confirmed. It is written from an Anglican perspective, and covers most subjects that new Christians need to learn or to discover for themselves.

This book can be used by individuals on their own, or by the group as a whole. In the latter case each individual will need a copy of the *Confirmation Book for Adults*. There is material that can be used for personal worship and study at home, as well as together with the group. Some of the suggestions under 'Further work' are contemplative, some creative, and individuals may like to carry out *some* of the tasks on their own. Group leaders may also find it useful to look at some of the 'Further work' with the whole group. No individual is expected to carry out all the tasks under 'Further work'.

The course is intended for adults, but selective material could easily be used by teenagers, or with a group of adults and teenagers. The 'Research' work is for those who would like to dig deeper, who may already have done some Christian study or academic work before, and who would benefit from something more challenging! This will not be suitable for everyone.

It is not necessary for the individual or the group to cover every subject in the book before the Confirmation. Some would be better looked at after the actual Confirmation service, e.g. Chapter 11, 'Living as a Christian'. Material could also be given to group members to look at between sessions.

Introduction

Each session in the book offers some Bible study, to allow those using the book to find out more about the Bible and how it can help them in their new life. As well as this there are a few suggestions for worship, which could be used alone or as the basis of some closing worship for the group.

In the Appendix are some suggestions for books that might be used to help while using the *Confirmation Book for Adults*.

Part 1

BEGINNINGS

BEGINNINGS

1

God calls us

Becoming a Christian is a personal decision for each individual to make, and everyone will have a different story to relate about what led up to the decision and how it was made. Some will have been 'Christened' as a baby and taken to church each week. They will have been encouraged by parents and godparents, and brought up in the faith throughout their childhood. Others may have chosen to reject God at an early stage and only begun to think about him during a difficult time in life, perhaps because of an illness or the death of a loved one. Some may have decided to keep their options open, perhaps because their parents believed that they should make their own life choices, but turned to God at a happy time in life, at their marriage or at the birth of a child. Others can identify the exact moment when they accepted God into their lives. The one thing all these have in common is that each individual was *called by God*.

For many people the process of becoming a Christian actually takes place slowly, almost unnoticed, over many years. God continues to call them again and again in very many different ways, throughout their life. Sometimes the call is not recognized, while at other times it can be deliberately ignored. Whatever our response, though, God continues to call us, hoping that we will turn to him. In the Bible we see God continually calling his people.

Bible work

Notice how many different ways God finds to get people's attention, and the way that individuals respond to him:

- Genesis 12.1–4: Abram.
- 1 Samuel 3.1–10: Samuel.
- Isaiah 6.1–8: Isaiah.
- Matthew 1.20–23 and 2.13: Joseph.
- Luke 1.26–38: Mary.
- Matthew 9.9: Matthew.
- John 1.43–51: Philip and Nathanael.

In the past men and women have heard God's voice in their dreams or through the visitation of a messenger. Others have heard an actual voice. Like us, some have questioned the authenticity of the call, while others have ignored the message. Some, however, did respond to God's call and went on to become patriarchs (those earliest Fathers of the Church in the Old Testament), prophets (who sought to keep the Jewish nation true to their call from God) and disciples (who followed Jesus' command to take the good news of the gospel to the whole world).

Hearing God's call today

Today, God still calls his people. It can be hard to recognize his call, however, and sometimes we can only see the touch of his hand in retrospect when we look back at the events in our lives. Perhaps we can see it in the time we chose an unexpected path, or when a disaster ultimately turned into a triumph. Whether or not we actually recognize God's call, he continues to call us in many different ways. Just as in the past, God may call us through the influence of others, through his word in the Bible as we read it or hear it preached in church, through our conscience, through the grandeur or beauty of the natural world, and of course he may call us through prayer.

Over the centuries millions of Christians have heard the call from God, each in their own unique way. Two who spoke about their experience of being called are St John of the Cross in the sixteenth century, and C. S. Lewis in the twentieth century. Each responded differently.

- St John of the Cross noted that God met us halfway, reminding us of the way the Prodigal or Lost Son (Luke 15.11–24) is welcomed back by his father, who comes out to greet him before his son has arrived home and even before he has asked for his forgiveness: 'O Lord, my God, who will seek you with simple and pure love, and not find that you are all one can desire, for you show yourself first and go out to meet those who seek you?' (*The Collected Works of St John of the Cross*, Washington, DC, ICS Publications, 1991, p. 85)
- C. S. Lewis, on the other hand, decided that he believed in God because of his own powers of deduction. He simply could not explain the creation of the world in any other way: 'I arrived where I now am, not by reflection alone, but by reflection on a particular current experience. I am an empirical theist. I have arrived at God by induction.' (William Griffin, *C. S. Lewis: The authentic voice*, Oxford, Lion, 1986, p. 72)

The call is always tailored to us. For C. S. Lewis, the way to God came through intellectual argument!

What God's call brings

In ordinary life when someone calls us there is often a task associated with the call. Whether it is a friend ringing to ask whether we can drive him to the garage to pick up his car, or a member of the family wanting us to help celebrate her birthday, the call frequently requires a response from us. So it is when God calls us. When he calls, he usually has a job for us to do. The call rarely comes in isolation. For example, the disciples were called to take the good news of the gospel to the world. In the twenty-first century, Christians too are called to be God's people in order to share with the world the good news of Jesus Christ.

In many instances, the call will also bring with it a more specific job. Very often we may feel we are not capable of carrying out the task, but God knows when we are ready to do his work and we need to learn to trust his judgement. Moses was called to lead the Israelites, even though he was a poor speaker and felt totally unable to do the job. He explains this to God, only for God to find a solution to his problem:

> What of your brother Aaron the Levite? I know that he can speak fluently . . . You shall speak to him and put the words in his mouth; and I will be with your mouth and with his mouth, and will teach you what you shall do.
>
> (Exodus 4.14–15)

In the New Testament, similarly, the disciples are given a job. Jesus sends them out to take the good news to the people:

> Then Jesus called the twelve together and gave them power and authority over all demons and to cure diseases, and he sent them out to proclaim the kingdom of God and to heal . . . They departed and went through the villages, bringing the good news and curing diseases everywhere.
>
> (Luke 9.1–2, 6)

Jesus appears to give the disciples this task early in their ministry, not long after their call to follow him. They too would surely have lacked confidence in their ability to carry out the task, yet they obey Jesus' command and proclaim the Kingdom of God to the people. The lesson we should learn from these two stories is that those who are called by God will be given the necessary gifts to carry out the task.

The Confirmation group

Although we are personally called, and we make an individual decision to become a Christian, Christianity is essentially a corporate faith. It is simply not possible to be a Christian alone, for we must travel with others on our journey of life, and we need the companionship of others to continue to grow spiritually. We need to 'rub off our sharp edges' against other people. We must learn to help others as well as learn from them, in order that we ourselves and the whole Christian community may continue to grow more God-like.

Those who come for Confirmation usually explore their faith together in a Confirmation group. The group may meet for a few weeks, or may spend months together. Sometimes those who are preparing for Confirmation will stay together as a 'home' or 'cell' group after the Confirmation. The group may include adults and teenagers, and there may be a wide age range, as well as an even wider range of experience. It must be noted that those with the most life experience may not necessarily be the most spiritually mature! The child looking at a caterpillar will see the insect in a way that an adult, rushing to do the next piece of work that day, will fail to see. She will notice the colours, the shape, the articulated body of the caterpillar, and find awe in the small. Age does not necessarily mean we are closer to God: we may have been ignoring God's call for a long time!

Take the opportunity to learn from one another, as well as to encourage and pray for other members of the group. Explore your own beliefs and doubts, and share them with other group members, remembering always to keep confidences within the group!

Practical things

It will be useful to have a notebook, not least to jot down the names and phone or e-mail addresses of those in the group, and also a modern translation of the Bible. Different translations of the Bible can be used for different things. Sometimes we want the beauty of the King James edition, say at Christmas time when we want to hear the traditional words, but it will be easier to use a more modern translation to do some Bible study. Check with the group leader in case he or she would prefer the whole group to use a specific translation.

At the beginning of the course do some thinking and ask yourself:

- Why have I joined this group?
- What do I want out of the course?
- What would I like to ask?
- What weaknesses do I bring to the group?
- What strengths do I bring to the group?

Set yourself a task for the first meeting of the Confirmation group – to remember everyone's name and something about them. Christians endeavour to live for others rather than themselves, and to put selfish desires on one side. Being concerned for others, and praying for them, will become second nature in time. Praying for others must start with getting to know them.

Further work

Look at some of the tasks below, either on your own or as a group. It is not necessary to carry out all the tasks.

- Create a 'lifeline' – a line from left to right on a piece of paper, showing the highs and lows of events in your life from birth to the present time as peaks and troughs.
- Go back over the lifeline identifying times when God was felt to be present, or absent. Draw a new line to create fresh peaks and troughs. Do the two coincide, or are they different? What can you learn from the result?
- Do you think God has been calling you over the years? Can you identify any specific times or occasions when you believe he has called you? What was your response?
- Was there an 'important adult' in your early life, from whom you learnt about God? What did you learn from him or her?
- When did you first go to a church? Can you remember the occasion, how it felt, and what happened?
- Has anything happened recently to make you turn towards God?
- Wordsworth says:

> . . . I have felt
> A presence that disturbs me with the joy
> Of elevated thoughts; a sense sublime
> Of something far more deeply interfused,
> Whose dwelling is the light of setting suns . . .
> (from 'Lines Composed a Few Miles
> above Tintern Abbey')

Have you had an experience of God's presence in the natural world? What effect did it have on you? Where do you feel closest to God?
- Look at Matthew 7.7–8. How hard have you 'knocked at the door' or searched for God? Be honest!

Research

This section is for those who have perhaps already attended other courses, and who would benefit from 'digging deeper' and who might enjoy some more academic work.

- Discover the five classical arguments put forward for the existence of God by Thomas Aquinas: look them up on the Internet. Can you believe in them?
- Find out about the 'patriarchs': use an encyclopedia of the Bible (see Appendix) or look them up on the Internet.

Prayer and reflection

Light a candle, and use an icon or flowers as a focal point for worship. Look up one or more of the readings, then say the prayer *(either singly, if you are on your own, or plurally, if together)*, leaving space between the sentences to allow for meditation. Alternatively, reflect on the nature of your 'call' to be a Christian; leave space to listen to God and invite him into your life now.

Readings for worship
- Psalm 139.1–18.
- Matthew 7.7–8.
- Luke 15.11–24.

God,
We/I give you thanks that you have
cared for *us/me* from *our/my* birth . . .
We/I thank you that you have called
us/me to be your own and that *we/I*
have heard your call . . .
You have taught *us/me* that when *we/I*
knock the door will be opened . . .
We/I ask you to come closer to *us/me and
to each other* . . .
through Jesus Christ, our Lord. Amen.

God calls us

Sing *(if using this material in a group)* one of the following:

- 'Be still, for the presence of the Lord'
- 'God has chosen me'
- 'Jubilate, everybody'

Close by saying these words from Isaiah:

> Do not fear, for I have redeemed you;
> I have called you by name, you are mine.
> (Isaiah 43.1b)

or say the words of the Grace:

> The grace of the Lord Jesus Christ, the love of God, and the
> communion of the Holy Spirit be with all of *us/me*.
> (2 Corinthians 13.13)

BEGINNINGS

2

First contact with God: Baptism

The first formal contact that many people have with God is at their own Baptism (or 'Christening' as it is often called). Often this is within a few months of birth, and the adult will have no memory of this life-changing event. Sometimes adults are left feeling cheated that they had no choice in the matter, and ask their parish priest to re-baptize them. However, Baptism is a once-for-all event. After all, you only join a family once!

Adults baptized as children are already members of God's new family, the Church. God has been involved in their lives initially through their parents and godparents, who made promises on their behalf at their Baptism to bring them up as a Christian. Many adults will therefore have been nurtured in the faith throughout their child-hood and teenage years. *All* this time God has continued to call them, and now as adults they have answered God's call, and come to the point where they are ready to make their own considered commitment to God and to his Church.

For those who have not been baptized in infancy, God has called them as adults to take a first step towards him at Baptism, before going on to their Confirmation. In this case Baptism and Confirmation usually take place in the same service.

But if Baptism is often the first formal contact we have with God, this does not explain why we seek to be baptized. What are the reasons for being baptized?

Separation from God

To answer this question we need to look at our relationship with God. Christians believe that human beings are made in God's image. We are 'stamped with his mark' and have the ability to love, just as he loves us. The first Epistle of John teaches us that 'love is from God; everyone who loves is born of God and knows God', and that 'God is love, and those who abide in love abide in God, and God abides in them' (1 John 4.7, 16b).

More than this, God wants to have a relationship with us in the same way that he does with Jesus. But the trouble is that although humans have the ability to love they also have a predisposition towards evil: to engage with the things that destroy all the good that God wants for them. We only have to look at our world to see how things have gone wrong. War, murder and exploitation are seen nightly on our television screens. Even the best of us can be selfish or unkind, or find it difficult to love others. This is the effect of sin, which in itself is the result of our estrangement from God.

However, as well as the sin that we commit daily, the Church believes in what St Paul calls 'original sin'. The basis of original sin is the Fall: that is, the story of Adam and Eve (see Genesis 2 and 3). Created perfect, Adam and Eve chose to go their own way, and in doing so introduced death and disorder into the world. All humans are born into this state of sin (as distinct from actual sin that we all commit), and because of this they are unable to have a loving relationship with God or with one another. As St Paul says, 'sin came into the world through one man, and death came through sin, and so death spread to all because all have sinned' (Romans 5.12). This understanding of original sin is held by many in the Methodist Church today. On the other hand, Roman Catholics would want to argue that though original sin has tarnished the original goodness of humanity, it has not entirely extinguished that goodness.

St Augustine of Hippo (AD 354–430), one of the most important figures in the development of Christianity, argued that even though a baby had not actually sinned, he or she was nevertheless subject to sin. The child is born into a broken and divided world where sin is already active and human nature is flawed. He or she is influenced by the actions of others and by choices made by them.

Many Christians today, of course, would argue that modern theories of evolution (like the 'big bang') have challenged Christian belief in the historical accuracy of the story of Adam and Eve. Although some fundamentalists still understand the story of Adam and Eve to be about historical people and about an event that essentially changed human beings, far more now understand the story to be about basic truths. Along with a number of other stories in the Old Testament, the story of Adam and Eve is there to help us understand the importance and truth about sin and human rebellion from God, regardless of historical accuracy. The Fall is seen as a sign of the choices that we all have to make in our ordinary lives.

Whether or not Adam and Eve are considered to be historical fact or metaphor, only God's loving grace can rescue us from our separation from him and effect our salvation. We are unable to help ourselves. Christians therefore believe that Jesus has atoned for original sin through his death and resurrection; that God has effected his saving plan to reunite us to himself, through his Son, Jesus Christ (see Ephesians 1.10). Our salvation occurs by faith alone (*sola fide*) and by grace alone (*sola gratia*); that is, our salvation occurs because of our faith in Jesus, and because of God's grace in seeking to rescue us. God brings us back into relationship with himself because of his love for us, and he seeks to rescue us (Ephesians 2.4–10) through the sacrifice of his Son, Jesus, on the cross (Colossians 2.13–15).

The reconciliation of God and man, through Jesus Christ, is called by the Church 'atonement'.

Why Baptism?

Baptism is the way that we show we have entered into a new relationship with God. Put simply, Baptism is the formal beginning of our life of faith. It is also a sign of God's love for us and his involvement in our life. In Baptism the person (or parents and god-parents on behalf of a child) turns away from his or her old life of selfishness and sin, and promises to live a new life following God's ways. In Baptism our real and actual day-to-day sins are washed away. In doing so the person is adopted into God's new family, the Church, and is brought within the love and care of that Church to be nurtured in growth as a Christian.

In the Baptism service the priest says to the congregation, and to the candidate:

> Our Lord Jesus Christ has told us
> that to enter the kingdom of heaven
> we must be born again of water and the Spirit,
> and has given us baptism as the sign and seal of this new
> birth.
> Here we are washed by the Holy Spirit and made clean.
> Here we are clothed with Christ,
> dying to sin that we may live his risen life.
> As children of God, we have a new dignity
> and God calls us to fullness of life.
>
> (*Common Worship*)

Baptism completes initiation into God's new family. However, there is a need for those who are baptized as children to take the promises made at Baptism for themselves. This occurs at Confirmation, which may take place many years afterwards. Initially Confirmation would have been part of a wider cere-mony of Christian initiation, which became separated when the Church grew and the bishop could no longer attend all Baptisms.

At Confirmation the promises made by parents and godparents are taken by the adult. It is not reasonable, after all, to expect an adult to abide by promises made by others on his or her behalf. The bishop asks God to strengthen or 'confirm' his involvement with the candidate's life which was originally made at Baptism. Where Baptism and Confirmation occur in the same service, the two parts taken together complete the acceptance of the adult into God's family, the Church.

Symbolism in Baptism

The Baptism service is full of symbolism. Most of what is said and done in the service has multiple layers of meaning. Symbolism underscores much of the service, and many people will continue to discover different layers of meaning over the years as they reflect on what is happening during the service. For example, the water, the sign of the cross 'drawn' on the candidate's forehead, and the light of the candle are all symbolic. These are outward symbols of things that the Church hopes will be experienced inwardly by every baptized person.

Symbols of Baptism

- *Water*: the child or adult is either fully immersed into water or sprinkled with water. The amount of water does not matter for the symbolism to work! Water 'washes' away all that stops us from restoring our relationship with God, and makes us pure before God. Water also refreshes us, as when we drink a glass of water on a hot day, and water continues to sustain us throughout our life. In Baptism we start our life again, restored, renewed and refreshed. Water is also dangerous and causes many deaths. So in Baptism water is a symbol of drowning or burial, and is linked to Jesus' death. In the Baptism service the priest stands before the water of Baptism and says:

  We thank you, Father, for the water of baptism.
  In it we are buried with Christ in his death.

  In Baptism we speak of the end of our old life and the beginning of a new one, just as though we have died and

---

The special relationship

At Baptism, God and the new Christian are committed to each other in a special relationship. In effect, a contract is drawn up between the two, rather like the 'contract' made in a marriage, where each promises to love and cherish the other. In the Old Testament such contracts or 'covenants' were often drawn up between people to establish a new relationship between them. A 'covenant' is an agreement made between equals. In the Old Testament (and in Baptism) a contract is made where God becomes the God of an individual or a nation, and they become his people. God chooses to make himself equal to those he has created, and each party to the contract then makes promises to the other.

---

been born again. The priest, referring to the water of Baptism, says:

> Through it [i.e. the water] we are reborn by the Holy Spirit.

He or she asks God to sanctify the water so that the candidates may be 'cleansed from sin and born again'.

- *The cross*: the cross that is made on our forehead (sometimes with oil or else with water) 'labels' us as belonging to God's Son, Jesus Christ, for ever. It was by dying on the cross that Jesus paid the penalty for humanity's wrong choices, so that these can no longer spoil our relationship with God. So in Baptism we become God's people.
- *The lighted candle*: the candle reminds us that we have passed from a dark world, where sin rules, to a world of light where we are accepted as we really are – warts and all – and where we can find forgiveness for our sins through Jesus.

Bible work

Look up these examples of covenants in the Old Testament. Can you see both sides of the contract? What is promised?

- Genesis 22.1–18: Abraham.
- Genesis 9.8–17: Noah.
- Genesis 28.10–22: Jacob.
- Exodus 3 and 4: Moses.

At the Baptism of a child the parents and godparents make a similar contract with God, but in this case on behalf of the child. The Baptism is carried out because of their faith. They promise to pray for the child, and to draw the child by their own life and example into the worship of the Church. At Baptism, the parents of a child and any adults who are to be baptized choose to ally themselves with Jesus Christ:

- to 'turn to Christ as Saviour';
- to 'submit to Christ as Lord';
- to 'come to Christ, the way, the truth and the life'.

Promises asked at Baptism

- Do you reject the devil and all rebellion against God?
- Do you renounce the deceit and corruption of evil?
- Do you repent of the sins that separate us from God and neighbour?
- Do you turn to Christ as Saviour?
- Do you submit to Christ as Lord?
- Do you come to Christ, the way, the truth and the life?

Accepting that we sin, and that in doing so we reinforce our separation from God, the first three questions at the Baptism service ask whether we are willing to align ourselves with God and reject all that is not good for us. If we answer in the affirmative, this means we choose to turn away from those personal temptations that attract us, as well as from the more obvious large-scale sins like theft or murder. This is our moment to make a stand and to make a decision that will affect our whole life. From now on, we are to live a new life, following the commandments of God:

The Ten Commandments

God gave the Israelites Ten Commandments on tablets of stone:

- I am the Lord your God: you shall have no other gods but me.
- You shall not make for yourself any idol.
- You shall not dishonour the name of the Lord your God.
- Remember the Sabbath and keep it holy.
- Honour your father and your mother.
- You shall not commit murder.
- You shall not commit adultery.
- You shall not steal.
- You shall not bear false witness against your neighbour.
- You shall not covet anything which belongs to your neighbour.

(Common Worship)

The Great Commandment

When a lawyer asked him what he must do to inherit eternal life, Jesus gave his definition of the Commandments. We call this the 'Great Commandment':

You shall love the Lord your God with all your heart, and with all your soul, and with all your strength, and with all your mind; and your neighbour as yourself.

(Luke 10.27)

After we have answered the first three questions at Baptism, the last three questions are the corollary. Having agreed to turn our back on evil, we are now asked whether we are willing to identify ourselves with the person of Jesus. Christians are essentially in a special relationship with Jesus. It is not enough just to believe in God as our Father. We have to believe that his Son, Jesus, is our Saviour, and we can only make sense of that if we understand that our wrong choices have caused us to be separated from a loving and perfect God. Every sin we commit further separates us from God. However, Jesus found a solution to our problem and offers us a way out of the dilemma. Christians believe that Jesus died for *our sins*, not because of *his sins*. He was sinless. In other words, Jesus died for our sake and on our behalf, and in doing so he re-established our right relationship with God. God the Father did not ask this of his Son, Jesus; it was offered out of love for us.

Our response to this amazing free offer of love (or 'grace', as St Paul calls it in his letters) is to confess our sin, and to submit to his loving rule for the rest of our lives. As a result of these public affirmations, the newly baptized person is to be a follower of Jesus Christ, i.e. a 'Christian'. His or her future life is to be a mirror image of the life that Jesus would be living if he were still walking among us on earth today as a man.

Baptisms in the early Church

Today we prepare Baptism candidates through an interview or sometimes classes (for parents and godparents), or through an adult Confirmation course. In the New Testament Baptism was one of the earliest signs of conversion. Those who repented of their sins accepted the Lord Jesus into their lives, and were immediately baptized.

In the early Church, candidates for Baptism were prepared over months or even years. In the Church in Rome in AD 200 the candidates were 'washed' in the name of the Father, the Son and the Holy Spirit, and anointed with oil after a strenuous Lent when they had been separated from their family and the congregation to be taught about their new faith. The climax of the preparation came on Easter Eve when they were baptized, and then immediately Confirmed. After that the new Christians, clothed in pristine white, received Communion for the first time at the Easter Eucharist. At this point in the Church's life, Baptism and Confirmation had not become separated.

Bible work

Look up the account of these Baptisms in the New Testament. What are the differences between them? How do they equate with Baptisms today?

- The Baptism of Jesus: Mark 1.9–11.
- The disciples baptize the first Christians: Acts 2.37–41.
- The Baptism of the Ethiopian eunuch: Acts 8.26–38.
- The conversion and Baptism of Saul: Acts 9.1–19a.

Further work

- If you were baptized as a child, what benefits do you think this has had? Has it helped, or even hindered, your life as a Christian? Find out all about your own Baptism – where and when did it take place?
- Attend a Baptism service and make a note of the symbolism that occurs, both in the language of the service and in the ritual movement and action.
- Think about the everyday uses of water, and make a list of all of them. Then think about the symbolic use of water as a Christian. Spend a few moments concentrating on the things you have done wrong, and finally ask God to 'wash away your sin' and to forgive you the wrong choices you have made.
- Look at the first three promises made in the Baptism service. Then privately write down three areas of your life where you consider you are not living the life that God requires. How could

you make changes to your life? Keep a note of your thoughts, and periodically check whether you are making any progress.

• Think about the symbolism of light in the Baptism service. Light a candle and look at the light. Jot down any words that come into your mind when you look at the candle (these may be symbolic or factual, e.g. 'flame'). What do you think it means to say 'Jesus is the Light of the world'? Jot down words that come into your mind when you think of Jesus as the 'Light of the world'.

Research

• Find out how members of the Baptist Church are received into the Church as children, and when and how they are baptized as adults. If possible, attend a Baptism service in a Baptist church. Then compare the service to that found in the Church of England's *Common Worship*.

Prayer and reflection

Light a candle, and use an icon or flowers as a focal point for worship. Look up the readings, and use the prayer from the *Common Worship* Baptism service below.

Reflect on the nature of being born as a baby – how might it feel? Equate this to being born again as a new Christian at Baptism.

Alternatively, reflect on those you know who were baptized as babies but who have not followed up that call, and pray for them. Pray for all parents and godparents.

Readings for worship
• Acts 10.44–48.
• Matthew 3.11–12.

Sing one of these:

- 'The Spirit lives to set us free'
- 'Seek ye first the Kingdom of God'

> Heavenly Father,
> by the power of your Holy Spirit
> you give to your faithful people
>   new life in the water of baptism.
> Guide and strengthen us by the same Spirit,
> that we who are born again may
>   serve you in faith and love,
> and grow into the full stature of
>   your Son, Jesus Christ,
> who is alive and reigns with you
>   in the unity of the Holy Spirit
> now and for ever. Amen.
>
> (*Common Worship*)

Part 2

CHRISTIAN BELIEF

CHRISTIAN BELIEF

3

What do I believe? God

———◆◆◆———

Most Christians if asked the question 'What do you believe about God?' would be unable to give a clear and concise answer. Perhaps the simplest of all answers is to say, 'God made the world.' Certainly this is how the Psalmists approached their belief in God. God, they believed, made the heavens and the earth, and was concerned with everything in his world. As Psalm 24 says:

> The earth is the LORD's and all that is in it,
> the world, and those who live in it;
> for he has founded it on the seas,
> and established it on the rivers.
>
> (Psalm 24.1–2)

The Creeds

After the death and resurrection of Jesus, and the establishment of the early Christian Church, it became important for Christians to decide exactly what they believed about God and about his Church. This period was dominated by the Apostolic Fathers, men like Clement I, Ignatius and Polycarp. Clement and Ignatius both stressed the need for order and ministerial succession in the Church, while Polycarp, the Bishop of Smyrna, gave instructions in his work the *Didache* for the conduct of Baptism and of the Communion service.

By the end of the second century, men like Justin Martyr, Irenaeus and Tertullian were writing apologetic works to defend the faith. Justin argued that Jesus was the eternal Word, the Son of God (see John 1.1–14), while Irenaeus argued against the Gnostics, who believed that God was spirit and totally remote from the physical world. The word 'Gnosticism' covers a number of different sects at this time who believed that though the body was physical the soul was divine. Their views meant that they considered Jesus to be totally human, and not divine. The early Fathers challenged these heretical views, believing that Jesus was both God and man.

By the fourth century the beliefs of the early Church had come together in a number of statements of belief, or Creeds. These are now used in worship in the Church throughout the world. The word 'creed' comes from '*credo*', or 'I believe' – the opening words of two of the most famous Creeds (see pp. 30–1).

The Nicene Creed is said during the service of Holy Communion and is one of the three major Creeds. It has been the result of considerable debate and even war in the past. The product of a Church Council held at Nicaea in Bithynia in AD 325, attended by over 300 bishops from around the world, this Creed attempts to answer the thorny question of how Jesus is both man and God. Notice how the word 'one' is repeated, and also how our present translation uses the phrase 'We believe' rather than 'I believe'. This is to be the Creed in which the whole Church corporately believes.

A second Creed, *the Apostles' Creed*, is used in the Baptism service as well as in Morning and Evening Prayer. This appeared a little later, around AD 400, although it wasn't finally completed until the eighth century. Together with the third creed, *the Creed of St Athanasius*, found in the Book of Common Prayer, it sought to answer questions that were perplexing the Church at the time it was written. For example, what exactly were Christians to believe? Was there one God or three Gods? What exactly did happen to Jesus after his death?

The Creeds state what the Church as a whole believes, that God created the world (in the Nicene Creed a role is given to Jesus), that he sent his Son, Jesus, to be born of Mary, and that he was crucified but rose again. The language is formal, as fits a statement to be read in public and one that has been created through such a tortuous method of revision. None of the Creeds argue for the existence of God: this is assumed. The believer is expected to have faith.

It is worth remembering that the Creeds state the Church's belief, not necessarily each individual's belief. For each of us there will be statements that we find easy to believe, and others that are more challenging and require greater study, prayer and faith if we are to accept them! There is nothing new in this. Christians have been 'growing into the Creeds' for many centuries. Compare the two Creeds on pp. 30 and 31.

Basic beliefs

Christians believe in God. As such they are theists. They are not atheists who deny the existence of God, neither are they agnostics who are uncertain whether or not there is a God. Not only do they believe in God, but they believe in *one* God. They, along with Jews and Muslims, are monotheists, denying the existence of other gods. As such the word 'God' is therefore always spelt with a capital G!

Indeed, God's name is so precious that the Jews refuse to use it. When Moses asked God for his name, God replied, 'I AM WHO I AM' (Exodus 3.14). This is one of only a few names that the Jews use for God. 'Yahweh' (or 'I AM WHO I AM') comes from the verb 'to be', and means 'to be active'. Another name is the plural word for God, 'Elohim', meaning 'one who possesses the divine attributes', and yet another is 'El Shaddai' or 'The Almighty'. A look at the Jerusalem translation of the Bible will show that the word 'Yahweh' is used for God in the Old Testament.

Although both the Old and New Testaments try to avoid using the name of God, they do use a number of graphic images to help describe and give a picture of God. In the book of Psalms alone, there are many different such descriptions of God.

Compare these two Creeds. What are the differences, and the similarities?

Nicene Creed

> We believe in one God,
> the Father, the Almighty,
> maker of heaven and earth,
> of all that is,
> seen and unseen.
>
> We believe in one Lord, Jesus Christ,
> the only Son of God,
> eternally begotten of the Father,
> God from God, Light from Light,
> true God from true God,
> begotten, not made,
> of one Being with the Father;
> through him all things were made.
> For us and for our salvation he came down from
>   heaven,
> was incarnate of the Holy Spirit and the Virgin Mary
> and was made man.
> For our sake he was crucified under Pontius Pilate;
> he suffered death and was buried.
> On the third day he rose again
> in accordance with the Scriptures;
> he ascended into heaven
> and is seated at the right hand of the Father.
> He will come again in glory to judge the living and
>   the dead,
> and his kingdom will have no end.
>
> We believe in the Holy Spirit,
> the Lord, the giver of life,

who proceeds from the Father and the Son,
who with the Father and the Son is worshipped and
   glorified,
who has spoken through the prophets.
We believe in one holy catholic and apostolic
   Church.
We acknowledge one baptism for the forgiveness of
   sins.
We look for the resurrection of the dead,
and the life of the world to come.
Amen.

Apostles' Creed

I believe in God, the Father almighty,
creator of heaven and earth.

I believe in Jesus Christ, his only Son, our Lord,
who was conceived by the Holy Spirit,
born of the Virgin Mary,
suffered under Pontius Pilate,
was crucified, died, and was buried;
he descended to the dead.
On the third day he rose again;
he ascended into heaven,
he is seated at the right hand of the Father,
and he will come to judge the living and the dead.

I believe in the Holy Spirit,
the holy catholic Church,
the communion of saints,
the forgiveness of sins,
the resurrection of the body,
and the life everlasting.
Amen.   (*Common Worship*)

31

Bible work

Look up these descriptions of God. How many other descriptions of God in the Bible can you find?

- God as a king: Psalm 46.
- God as Creator: Psalm 104.
- God as Judge: Psalm 82.
- God as a shepherd: Psalm 23.
- God as a rock, a fortress and a shield: Psalm 18.2.

Further beliefs about God

Christians believe not only that God made the world, but that he is *other* than the world. They do not believe in pantheism, where a god and the world are one. God chooses to reveal himself to his world through very normal ways, but supremely he reveals himself through his Son, Jesus. Our best description of God, and one that was used by Jesus himself, is of a loving Father, who cares for all his children, even when they turn away from him and commit sin. He reveals himself to his people as a *holy* God, a God who is perfect and who wants his children to live in love together. He longs for them to return to him, and to this end he sent his Son Jesus, to effect a rescue package.

Beliefs about God in the Bible

- God knows everything, he is *omniscient* (Psalm 139.1–4).
- God is all-powerful, he is *omnipotent*, he made the world (Psalm 8).
- God is everywhere, he is *omnipresent*, indwelling in the whole of his cosmos (Psalm 139.7–10).
- God is *transcendent*. He is other than his creation. He exists outside time and space (Revelation 1.8).
- God is *Trinity*, one being but three persons, Father, Son and Holy Spirit (John 14.15–17).

Two other aspects of God are not included in the Creed. First, God is *unchanging*. He is the same yesterday and today, and will be the same tomorrow. Because of this we can trust him and his promises absolutely. Second, if we believe that God is other than his creation and if he exists outside time and space, then he is also *eternal*.

The question of suffering

One question that causes many people problems, and one of the reasons why some cannot answer God's call to become one of his family, concerns suffering. If God is all-loving and cares for us, why does he allow suffering in the world? Well, there is no absolute answer to this question, at least not this side of death, when we may know much more of God's plans for our world. However, there are some things to consider:

- Natural disasters are often caused by human intervention, e.g. floods are sometimes caused by deforestation on mountainsides, or by people building on flood plains.
- Our world is continuing to grow and change. It is not a static world, and we choose to live in inappropriate places, e.g. close to volcanoes or above the rift caused by the collision of tectonic plates.
- Human beings often inflict misery and suffering on each other through their selfishness. Much of the suffering in our world is caused by humans, e.g. war, murder, theft, death by dangerous driving, and rape.
- We are not puppets. We have been given free will, and because of this we choose to do good or evil during our time on earth.

God is not indifferent to our suffering. Neither does he deliberately cause suffering. God loves all his creation. He allowed himself to be known to his people through his Son, Jesus, who was subject to torture and death. God himself knows what it is to suffer. However, he has shown us that new life can come from death, through resurrection.

Further work

- To the question 'God is . . . ?' what would you answer? What is God like? How many aspects of God can you list?
- Which aspects of God are most important to you?
- Try to imagine God, or draw him as an image. What might he look like?
- Consider God as a mother rather than a father. Are there any differences to your image?
- Look at the Nicene Creed in the Communion service from *Common Worship*. Can you identify with some of these statements, and are there other statements that cause you difficulty?
- What things do you believe in today in our world? Can you create a modern 'creed' for today's Christians, one that is positive and not negative?

Research

- Find out about either of these heresies: Arianism or Pelagianism. Why were they so dangerous to the early Church, and what occurred because of them? Use a book on early Church history, or look them up on the Internet.
- Are there heresies within the Church today? Look at any beliefs that do not fit a Trinitarian and loving God.

Prayer and reflection

Light a candle, and use a picture of some aspect of nature as a focal point for worship. Read through the words of the Nicene Creed.

Are there any areas of your belief that cause you problems? Ask God's help that you may continue to learn and grow in faith.

Slowly say the words of the Apostles' Creed aloud.

Readings for worship
- 1 Corinthians 15.3–7.
- Revelation 4.8–11.

Sing one of these:

- 'Abba Father'
- 'Be still and know that I am God'
- 'Come and praise the living God'
- 'Father, we love you'

Finally, close by thanking God for all that he has done for you, or by using these words:

> Lord, may this candle be a light for you to enlighten me in my difficulties.
> Lord, may it be a fire for you to burn out my selfishness and sin.
> Lord, may it be a flame to bring warmth into my heart towards my family, neighbours, and all whom I meet today.
> Lord, I cannot stay long here with you, but in lighting this candle I wish to give you something of myself this day. Amen.
>
> (Anon)

CHRISTIAN BELIEF

4

What is Christianity? Jesus Christ

At the heart of Christianity is a relationship. Christianity is not just about following a Creed or even a particular code of conduct. It is not just about worshipping God in a building, or using certain liturgical patterns. The essence of Christianity is Jesus Christ, God's Son, and our personal relationship with him as our Saviour and King.

God's relationship with his people

In the Old Testament we see God's relationship with the Jewish nation, a people who were the first to recognize that there was only *one* God. Other nations might worship gods of nature or the gods of their ancestors, but this small nomadic tribe came to realize that there was only one God.

More important still, God allowed himself to be known to his people. From Noah to Abram, Isaac and finally Moses, God made contracts or covenants with each of these tribal leaders. God would protect and care for his people if they would follow his commandments and worship him. There were frequently frustrations on both sides, rather like any parent-and-child relationship. When things got difficult the Jews turned away from God, and even began worshipping idols. But always God was there for them when they returned to him. From the exodus out of Egypt, through the 40 years in the desert, God nurtured the Jewish people, leading them to what was known as 'the Promised Land'.

The coming of the Messiah

Over the centuries God's people were also being prepared, through each tribulation, for the coming of the 'Messiah'. Slowly there grew up an expectation that one day God would send a Messiah to save his people from their enemies, like the Romans, who continued to oppress them. What kind of a person the Messiah would be was arguable. Some thought 'the Christ' (that is, the Messiah) would be a great warrior, rather like their ancestor King David, who would sweep the oppressors away. Others thought that he would be a priest or a prophet, rather like the great prophet Elijah, who would guide the people. Few noticed the writings of Isaiah, who spoke of a 'suffering servant' who would give up his life for the 'sin of many' (Isaiah 53.12).

Prophetic writings about the Messiah

These writings describe some of the expectations that existed about the kind of Messiah that the Jewish people believed would come to rescue God's people.

- Zephaniah 1.14: the day is near.
- Isaiah 11.1–5: a shoot from Jesse (King David's father).
- Isaiah 7.14: a child shall be born.
- Isaiah 53: the suffering servant.
- Micah 5.2: the king will be born in Bethlehem.
- Zechariah 9.9: the king will ride on a donkey.

After a gap of many centuries with no prophets appearing, John the Baptist, who was related to Jesus, began to focus the expectancy of the nation by calling the people to repentance and warning them of the imminence of the Messiah. John was to be the last great prophet, the 'forerunner' who would prepare the people for God's intervention into history in the shape of his Son, Jesus. Isaiah described the coming of this 'forerunner' in this way:

A voice cries out:
'In the wilderness prepare the way of the LORD,
make straight in the desert a highway for our God.'
(Isaiah 40.3)

Mark begins his Gospel by quoting words from Isaiah, and with John coming out of the wilderness, dressed in the traditional garb of a prophet. He appears like a bolt out of the blue, declaring:

> The one who is more powerful than I is coming after me; I am not worthy to stoop down and untie the thong of his sandals. I have baptized you with water, but he will baptize you with the Holy Spirit.　　　　(Mark 1.7–8)

To emphasize this, Jesus promptly arrives from Nazareth in Galilee to be baptized by John in the River Jordan. This is great drama, and the Jews who knew their Scriptures responded in droves to John's rousing call.

Who was Jesus?

As can be seen from looking at the Creeds (see Chapter 3) there was to be controversy for many years about the question of 'Who was Jesus?' In one sense, however, it is easy to start by looking at the facts that we do know, rather than by starting with the ones that puzzle us. We can say from the Gospels, and from the evidence of men like Josephus, a first-century Jewish historian, that:

- Jesus was a man who was born in Bethlehem.
- He lived in Palestine over 2,000 years ago.
- His parents were Mary and Joseph, who was a carpenter.
- He had brothers and sisters.
- He lived most of his life in Nazareth.
- He started his work as a preacher, teacher and healer when he was around 30 years old.
- He gathered a group of disciples around him.

- He was handed over to his enemies and was crucified less than three years later, and buried in a borrowed tomb, guarded by Roman soldiers.
- He appeared to his followers three days later, saying he had 'arisen', and was seen by many hundreds of people.
- His followers, who were soon to be called 'Christians', spread the 'good news' of his resurrection throughout the world.

We can also say, with confidence, that Jesus was fully human. We have evidence in the Gospels, and in the early writings of the Church, that he lived in every sense the life of a man:

- He grew tired and sat down to rest (John 4.3–6).
- He suffered thirst, asking a woman at a well to give him a drink (John 4.7–8).
- He could take pity on the plight of the poor or the sick (Luke 7.11–15).
- He could be sad at the death of a loved one (John 11.32–36).
- He could get angry at those who sought to cheat others (Mark 11.15).

Jesus was in every sense a normal man. But we can also say much more about him.

Jesus the Son of God

What was different about Jesus was his relationship with God. In the account of Jesus' birth, Luke says:

> The angel said to her, 'Do not be afraid, Mary, for you have found favour with God. And now, you will conceive in your womb and bear a son, and you will name him Jesus.' . . . Mary said to the angel, 'How can this be, since I am a virgin?' The angel said to her, 'The Holy Spirit will come upon you, and the power of the Most High will overshadow you; therefore the child to be born will be holy; he will be called Son of God.'   (Luke 1.30–32, 34–35)

Matthew says:

> Mary had been engaged to Joseph, but before they lived
> together, she was found to be with child from the Holy Spirit.
>
> (Matthew 1.18)

Both these accounts record that Jesus was born by the action
of the Holy Spirit, with no human father involved. St Paul uses
language that indicates his belief in the Virgin Birth in 1 Corinthians 15.45–48, and after AD 100 some of the Apostolic Fathers,
Ignatius, Justin and Irenaeus among them, accept the Virgin
Birth. The Protestant Churches believe in the virginal conception
of Jesus through the power of the Holy Spirit, although some
Christians find this concept difficult and argue that the word for
virgin might merely mean a young girl.

During his ministry we see the way that Jesus' relationship to
God was different. He called God 'Father', or in his native language,
Aramaic, he used the diminutive word for father, which might be
the equivalent of 'Daddy' today. This relationship was unique. Jesus
taught his disciples that he was God's Son, saying: 'The Father and
I are one' (John 10.30), and that

> If I am not doing the works of my Father, then do not believe
> me. But if I do them, even though you do not believe me,
> believe the works, so that you may know and understand that
> the Father is in me and I am in the Father.
>
> (John 10.37–38)

In his relationship with God, Jesus showed us a new way to live.
He spent hours in solitude, praying to his Heavenly Father, and
took no major decisions without going aside to pray. At the beginning of his ministry he spent 40 days in retreat in the wilderness,
and before making his way back to Jerusalem at the close of his
work and to his likely death, he spent further time in prayer.

Jesus showed in his ministry an authority and power never seen
before. Whether or not we believe in some or all of the miracles

is not important. Miracles were seen as special *signs* of God's presence, and the important thing was to question what they meant, not whether they had actually happened. We see Jesus exercising authority and power:

- in healing (Mark 2.1–12; Luke 6.6–10);
- in calling people to follow him (Mark 2.13–17);
- in forgiving sin (Luke 5.17–26);
- over nature (Mark 4.35–41; John 2.1–11);
- over unclean spirits (Mark 5.1–13);
- over death (John 11.1–44; Matthew 9.18–25).

The teaching of Jesus

Jesus was proclaimed as a great teacher. He followed the traditions of his day, but he taught with authority, defining the nature of God's Kingdom and outlining the response that God expected from his people. The main theme of his ministry was: 'The time is fulfilled, and the kingdom of God has come near; repent, and believe in the good news' (Mark 1.15).

During his three years travelling through Palestine with his disciples, Jesus continually taught about 'God's Kingdom'. God's Kingdom was to be a Kingdom of peace and love, where men and women obeyed God's commands and allowed him into their lives. In his life and work Jesus showed us something of what a Kingdom of love and peace might be like. The widow and orphan would be cared for, and the poor and oppressed would be rescued.

Jesus taught his disciples that human beings are inherently sinful. We are often selfish, putting ourselves first and others second. Ultimately, this separates us from God, who is perfect. In his work with the poor, the sick and the outcast, we see something of the way that our world can be changed if we allow Jesus into our lives. The Kingdom of God on earth has begun, though it will not be here completely until Christ returns to earth at his Second Coming to judge the world.

God's Kingdom is like . . .

Jesus used parables to describe what the Kingdom of God would be like:

- mustard seed: Matthew 13.31–32;
- yeast: Matthew 13.33;
- treasure: Matthew 13.44;
- pearls: Matthew 13.45;
- a net: Matthew 13.47–50.

As well as speaking with authority, another characteristic of Jesus' work was to use *parables* in his teaching. The word 'parable' comes from the Greek *parabole*, meaning something that is placed side by side, to act as a comparison. Jesus used parables for different reasons, sometimes to help explain something to a wider audience, but also sometimes as a riddle or puzzle that would need explaining to the inner core of his followers. In the latter case, the parable would be explained to the disciples at a later time. The Parable of the Sower is a case in point (Mark 4.3–8).

Many of the parables told by Jesus deal with the Kingdom of God, but others challenge traditional assumptions about property or crime, and end with the words 'Go and do likewise', or 'Let anyone with ears, listen!' Frequently the parables challenge the ruling authorities by attacking those who adhere to the words of the Law rather than the spirit of the Law, and often they support outcasts or apparent sinners. The Pharisee and the Tax Collector (Luke 18.9–14) and the Good Samaritan (Luke 10.30–37) are two cases in point. In the first of these, most Jews would assume that the Tax Collector would be the sinner – after all, he was working for the hated Romans – and the Pharisee was a man trying to obey God's laws. In the Good Samaritan, again, it is the hated Samaritan (for the Samaritans had set up another temple to rival that in Jerusalem) that would surely be the person to ignore the wounded man, rather than the respected Levite and priest.

Jesus used parables to teach the people how they should obey God's laws, and by the time of his entry into Jerusalem the authorities were desperate to arrest him to remove such a dangerous influence from the scene.

The death and resurrection of Jesus

Christians do not worship a God who is removed from his people or who does not understand their suffering. God was prepared to send his Son, Jesus, to live and die among us. After three years of ministry and pursued by his enemies, who included the leaders of his own people, the Pharisees, Jesus' time on earth was almost at an end. After a final meal with his friends he was handed over to be tortured and killed by Roman soldiers, at the instigation of the chief priests.

For Christians, Jesus is the God who has suffered, but who understands our pain. He is the God who also continues to suffer because of our rejection of him, and our disobedience to his will. His loving sacrifice was costly, involving his death. Jesus died for us to repair the broken relationship between God and humanity, to bring about atonement (or 'at-one-ment') for our sins. God, our Maker, has given us all that we have, yet we choose to reject him. For this we deserve punishment, but Jesus chose to take our place and to suffer instead of us; he offered himself as a ransom to pay our freedom. As John says in his Gospel:

> For God so loved the world that he gave his only Son, so that everyone who believes in him may not perish but may have eternal life. (John 3.16)

If this had been the end of the story, if Good Friday had finished it all, then evil would seem to have won. However, the Gospels tell us that Jesus overcame death, defeating the evil that killed him, and showing the power and glory of God. He was seen alive on the third day by his disciples, still with the marks of suffering on his body.

One of the disciples, Thomas, who did not see him initially, refused to accept that he was alive, saying:

> Unless I see the mark of the nails in his hands, and put my finger in the mark of the nails and my hand in his side, I will not believe. (John 20.25b)

However, he was forced to accept, along with the other disciples, that Jesus had risen from the grave and was alive, after seeing the wounds on Jesus' body. Luke, in his second book, the Acts of the Apostles, tells us that

> until the day when he was taken up to heaven . . . he presented himself alive to them by many convincing proofs, appearing to them over the course of forty days and speaking about the kingdom of God. (Acts 1.2–3)

John, the Gospel writer, relates another incident after Jesus' death. He says the disciples were fishing in Galilee when Jesus appeared on the beach and helped them to cast their net straight into a shoal of fish, and

> When they had gone ashore, they saw a charcoal fire there, with fish on it, and bread. Jesus said to them, 'Bring some of the fish that you have just caught.' . . . Now none of the disciples dared to ask him, 'Who are you?' because they knew it was the Lord. (John 21.9–10, 12b)

John, in his last chapter but one, says:

> Now Jesus did many other signs in the presence of his disciples, which are not written in this book. (John 20.30)

The festival of Christ's birth at Christmas is important, but Christians are an Easter people. Belief in the resurrection is at the foundation of the Christian faith. It is the reason why the Church was established, and why the Gospels and Epistles were written. Christians celebrate Jesus' death and resurrection, worshipping a God who still lives, and rejoicing in the hope that we too will join him one day.

Bible work

Read about the life and death of Jesus in the Gospels.

- Luke 1 and 2, and Matthew 1.18–2.23: the birth stories.
- John 1.35–51: the calling of the disciples.
- Luke 6.17–40: Jesus' teaching.
- Luke 15: the parables.
- Luke 9.12–17: a miracle.
- Mark 14.43–15.47: the death of Jesus.
- Luke 24.1–12: the resurrection.

Further work

- Read the whole of St Mark's Gospel. Jot down on a notepad examples of Jesus' miracles. Jesus says these are 'signs' that bear witness to the fact that God's Kingdom of love is at work in the world. How many different 'signs' can you find?
- Christians believe that 'where there is love, there is God'. Can you find any 'signs' of God's Kingdom of love at work in the world in the newspapers, or in the news, today?
- Look up the 'I am' sayings: John 6.35, 8.12, 10.7, 10.9, 10.11, 11.25, 14.6 and 15.1. Take one of these sayings and meditate on it each day this week.
- Read the different accounts of the resurrection in the four Gospels. They are naturally different because of different eye-witnesses. Do they have the ring of truth about them?
- Explore your local church looking for crosses. Crosses appear in many different shapes and sizes. Many have different names. You might like to find out about them.

- Read Luke 1.26–35. The Apostles' Creed (see Chapter 3) says that Jesus was 'conceived by the Holy Spirit' and 'born of the Virgin Mary'. Reflect on this. What do you feel about this statement?

Research

- Find out the exact meaning of the following words: incarnation, and atonement.
- Explore your local church looking for Christian symbols, e.g. a fish or a dove. Find out what they mean.
- Find out about Pierre Abélard and his notion that Christ's Passion was God suffering with his creatures in order to show the greatness of his love for them.

Prayer and reflection

Light a candle, and use an icon or flowers as a focal point for worship. Use the 'Jesus Prayer', saying it quietly over and over again: 'Lord Jesus Christ, Son of the Living God, have mercy on me, a sinner.'

Then take Jesus' last words on the cross and meditate on them:

> Father, into your hands I commend my spirit.
> (Luke 23.46)

Offer yourself into God's hands – all that is good and all that is bad in your life.

Readings for worship
- Philippians 2.5–8.
- John 15.1–7.

Sing one of the following:

- 'Alleluia, alleluia'
- 'Alleluia, alleluia, give thanks to the risen Lord'
- 'As we are gathered, Jesus is here'

Close with this prayer:

> Almighty Father,
> Look with mercy on this your family
> for which our Lord Jesus Christ was content to be
>   betrayed
> and given up into the hands of sinners
> and to suffer death upon the cross;
> who is alive and glorified with you and the Holy Spirit,
> one God, now and for ever. Amen.

CHRISTIAN BELIEF

5

The power of God: The Holy Spirit

———•◆•———

Having looked at *God as Father and Creator*, and at *God as his Son, Jesus Christ*, now we look at the third person of the Trinity, *God as the Holy Spirit* or the power of God. This is the aspect of God that we see at work in his Church and in the world today. These three aspects of God make up 'the Trinity', not three gods but one God: Father, Son and Holy Spirit.

The Spirit was at work before time existed, and evidence of his work can be seen throughout the Bible. The writer of Genesis in the King James translation speaks of the Spirit as 'brooding on the face of the waters' before the creation of the world. A newer translation puts it like this: 'the spirit of God swept over the face of the waters' (Genesis 1.2). In the book of Numbers the Spirit is seen with a new prophet as Moses is told by God to: 'Take Joshua son of Nun, a man in whom is the spirit, and lay your hands upon him' (Numbers 27.18). Later, in the book of Judges, the Spirit is seen as being with Samson from his youth:

> The woman bore a son, and named him Samson. The boy grew, and the LORD blessed him. The spirit of the LORD began to stir him . . .   (Judges 13.24–25a)

The Holy Spirit is worshipped as Lord, and is sometimes called 'the Spirit of God' or 'the Spirit of the Lord'.

Images for the Holy Spirit

As well as mentioning the Spirit by name, the Bible also offers us a number of images that denote the power of the Holy Spirit.

- The Spirit as a wind: Exodus 10.13, 19.
- The Spirit as a breath: Genesis 2.7b.
- The Spirit as silence: 1 Kings 19.12.
- The Spirit as a dove: Mark 1.10.
- The Spirit as a wind and tongues of fire: Acts 2.1–4.

The Spirit at Pentecost

Having completed the work that the Father had sent him to do, Jesus warned his disciples just before he left them that he would not be with them for ever. However, he promised that he would send 'the Comforter' and 'the Advocate', who would continue to work with them to help them proclaim the good news of God's Kingdom. After the resurrection Jesus told his disciples to stay in Jerusalem to wait for the promise of the Father for 'John baptized with water, but you will be baptized with the Holy Spirit' (Acts 1.5).

In the period after the resurrection, but before the coming of the Spirit at Pentecost, the disciples did as Jesus had asked and stayed in Jerusalem. They had hope, for they had seen Jesus alive after his death and he had promised that he would send the Holy Spirit to help them. He had talked with them, eaten with them, and then he had taken them outside the city and given them some last words. The disciples must have found it very hard to be without Jesus, and to live so close to the authorities that had crucified him. However, they waited patiently until the fiftieth day after the Passover at Pentecost. Then, when the disciples were all together in one room, the Holy Spirit came upon them. The description

of what happened is one of the most dramatic in the New Testament. Only Luke mentions this scene, in his second book, the Acts
of the Apostles, and he must have found it almost impossible to
describe what happened. Here are his words:

> When the day of Pentecost had come, they were all toge-
> ther in one place. And suddenly from heaven there came a
> sound like the rush of a violent wind, and it filled the entire
> house where they were sitting. Divided tongues, as of fire,
> appeared among them, and a tongue rested on each of
> them. All of them were filled with the Holy Spirit and began
> to speak in other languages, as the Spirit gave them ability.
>
> (Acts 2.1–4)

In the packed city there were men of all nationalities, and those
present were amazed that they could understand the disciples in
their own language. How could these uneducated men, with their
distinctive Galilean accents, speak so many languages? The event
was so dramatic that some onlookers assumed they were drunk,
for they seemed to them to be babbling. Peter had to exclaim that
they were not drunk for it was 'only nine o'clock in the morning'
(Acts 2.15).

This was only the first appearance of the Spirit in their lives,
only the first empowerment by God. In the first few chapters of
the Acts of the Apostles the Spirit is seen at work a number of
times, and the effect of the Spirit on the disciples is immediately
apparent. Peter, who had three times denied he knew Jesus before
the crucifixion, now has courage to stand up and address all the
people who are assembled. He is fluent, quoting prophecy from
Scripture, and testifying that Jesus has risen from the dead.
Suddenly an uneducated fisherman has become able to evangel-
ize a huge crowd. God's presence and power, through his Holy Spirit,
enables him to say:

Therefore let the entire house of Israel know with certainty that God has made him both Lord and Messiah, this Jesus whom you crucified. (Acts 2.36)

A few days later Peter and John, making their daily visit to the Temple, are faced with a lame beggar. Only a few weeks previously they had been unable to heal a young man at the foot of the mountain of transfiguration, but now Peter addresses the beggar with confidence:

'I have no silver or gold, but what I have I give you; in the name of Jesus Christ of Nazareth, stand up and walk' . . . and immediately his feet and ankles were made strong.
(Acts 3.6–7)

Inspired by the Holy Spirit, these men were bold enough to stand their ground and tell their listeners of the good news of Jesus Christ. They were bold enough, as with Stephen, to go to their deaths. The Holy Spirit had changed their lives for ever, and was to fill them with hope for the world to come. This was what led them to take the good news to the rest of the world.

The work of the Holy Spirit

The disciples must have wondered in those early days why it was necessary for Jesus to leave them. How could it be better when the Spirit came? However, the effect of the Holy Spirit was to universalize the work that Jesus had started. Now God's work was not restricted to a place and time in history. Through the Holy Spirit, Jesus could be with all his followers, then and in the future.

The Spirit could also enter the hearts of men and women and change them from within. As a man, Jesus was unable to do this, but the Spirit could enter the lives of individuals who had chosen to turn to God. St Paul was to pray for new converts in Ephesus:

that you may be strengthened in your inner being with
power through his Spirit, and that Christ may dwell in your
hearts through faith, as you are being rooted and grounded
in love.   (Ephesians 3.16b–17)

The coming of the Holy Spirit was the next phase in God's plan
for his people. His power was to be unleashed upon the disciples
to build God's new Church throughout the world.

What the Spirit brings

As we have seen, the Holy Spirit brought specific gifts to the
disciples and to all those who received the Spirit in the early days
of the Church and to those who have received him today. The
Church has traditionally spoken of these as the 'sevenfold gifts' or
'charismatic gifts' of the Holy Spirit. The sevenfold gifts are based
on the words of Isaiah, who prophesied that the Messiah would
come from the tribe of David, and that:

> The spirit of the LORD shall rest on him,
> the spirit of wisdom and understanding,
> the spirit of counsel and might,
> the spirit of knowledge and the fear of the LORD.
> His delight shall be in the fear of the LORD.
>
> (Isaiah 11.2–3)

The sevenfold gifts traditionally benefit the Church, and not the
individual who receives them. At Pentecost the sevenfold gifts gave
the disciples all the strength they needed to do God's work in the

world, and to initiate Christ's Church. Today the Spirit still brings gifts to individuals, for God's work:

- *wisdom* to see things the way that God does;
- *understanding* of what God wants;
- *counsel* to help us to know what to do when things are difficult;
- *inward strength* to live in the way we know God wants us to live;
- *knowledge* of the truth as revealed in Jesus;
- *true godliness* to live in a holy relationship with God as our Father and with others as our brothers and sisters;
- *fear of the Lord* to enable us to respond to God and giving us a fear that we may be separated from him.

Everyone who has been baptized has already received the first gift of the Spirit, by becoming a Christian. We need to pray for more gifts of the Spirit in order to carry out God's work in his world.

The fruits of the Spirit

If the Holy Spirit brings the Church the sevenfold gifts, he also brings to different individuals his 'fruits'. In the same way that a healthy tree will produce healthy fruit, so a healthy Christian will produce healthy spiritual fruit in his or her life. It is not enough to say we are Christians and believe in God. We must also show evidence of that belief in our lives, for 'just as the body without the spirit is dead, so faith without works is also dead' (James 2.26).

St Paul teaches that the fruits of the Spirit are:

love, joy, peace, patience, kindness, generosity, faithfulness, gentleness, and self-control. (Galatians 5.22)

Each of us will find some of the 'fruits' more difficult to achieve than others, and will need to pray about receiving them. We cannot hope to achieve them on our own, but with the help of the Holy Spirit we shall continue growing as Christians!

Bible work

Look up the following readings, concerning the Holy Spirit. What can you learn about the Spirit?

- Genesis 1.2: the Spirit at creation.
- 1 Kings 19.12: a sound of sheer silence (a still, small voice in some translations).
- Joel 2.28: prophecy that the Spirit would be given to all.
- Luke 1.26–35: Mary conceives by the Spirit.
- Matthew 3.13–17: the Spirit as a dove.
- John 14.25–26: the Spirit as the Advocate.
- Acts 2.1–13: the Spirit at Pentecost.
- Romans 8.14: the Spirit leads the children of God.
- 1 Corinthians 12.4–11: the gifts of the Spirit.
- Galatians 5.22–26: the fruits of the Spirit.

Further work

- Look back over your own life (or the lifeline that you did in the first week), and identify where the Holy Spirit has been at work in your life. Then identify areas of your life that need help. Ask the Holy Spirit for help.
- Examine the 'fruits of the Spirit' (Galatians 5.22–26). What 'fruits' has the Spirit given to you? Be honest! What 'fruits' do you need? Ask the Holy Spirit for help.
- Think about the other members of the Confirmation group. What 'fruits' of the Spirit have been distributed among the members? Give thanks for these!
- Create some collage work, or a painting, using some of the images of the Holy Spirit.
- Buy or make a symbol of a dove to hang in your home.
- Go and visit a 'charismatic' church, and if possible experience 'speaking in tongues' or 'healing'. What do you feel about these?

- Spend some time thinking about where the Holy Spirit is working in your church. Pray for this.

Research

- Find out about the gifts (not the fruits) of the Spirit that are given to people to use for God's work (see 1 Corinthians 12.4–11). Do you think God might be developing you in some way to work for his Church?

Prayer and reflection

Light a number of candles, to remind you of the Holy Spirit as a flame.

Reflect on the wind, and on its power and strength. We never see the wind itself, only its effect. It can be a breath or it can be a hurricane. The Holy Spirit comes unseen, but his effect can also be transformational in the life of individuals and in the Church.

Readings for worship

- Romans 8.26.
- 1 John 4.13.

Sing one of these:

- 'Breathe on me, breath of God'
- 'The Spirit lives to set us free'
- 'Spirit of the living God'

Use a newspaper to look at issues in the world that need prayer. List these, and ask the Holy Spirit for help, ending with 'if you will'.

CHRISTIAN BELIEF

6

Books to help: The Bible

The Bible is the most sold book in the world, if not necessarily the most read book. It has been produced in many different translations and many different languages. It has been described as 'God's Reference Library' and is not a book as such, but rather a library of books. Essentially it is divided into three main sections:

- the Old Testament: the Jewish scriptures, originally written in Hebrew;
- the Apocrypha: Jewish books, originally written in Greek;
- the New Testament: about Jesus and the new Church.

The Church of England uses the Old and New Testaments as well as the Apocrypha. However, it does not include the Apocrypha as part of its 'canon' (that is, the official books), unlike the Roman Catholic Church, which has always included the Apocrypha in the canon of the Church.

Within the Bible can be found books of history, law, hymns, wisdom, prophets, letters, love songs and poetry, written by many people over a period of a thousand years. All of them were written to show how God engaged with his people, how he nurtured and cared for them, how he chastised them, and finally how he rescued them. This is what is called 'Salvation History', and as such it is not concerned with the complete history of the Jewish people and their relations with other countries, or their economic or political history. It is history with a 'slant', looking at the religious history of the nation, and its relationship with God.

In order to understand Jesus and the early Church we need to make sense of the Old Testament, because for the early Church, and the Jews in particular, it was their sacred text. For Christians the whole Bible is 'God-breathed', and we can say that it has been inspired by God. It is important for us to make sense of the Old Testament if we are to understand exactly what Jesus has done for us, and to explore the New Testament, in order to see what message God has for us today. However, these books were not written by God: they were written by ordinary men and women, and they reflect the understanding and culture of their day. They have also been translated and copied over the centuries. As such they can, and do, contain mistakes.

The Old Testament

The Old Testament records God's dealings with the Jewish people, from their earliest beginnings as a small tribe, their establishment as a kingdom, their exile to Babylon, their final return to Jerusalem, and their rebuilding of the Temple. It tells the story of how God made an agreement (or 'covenant') with the early Fathers of the tribe, and how he guided and nurtured them over the years. It shows how the people ignored God's wishes and broke his rules again and again, and how he continued to call them back to him and to care for them.

The most important books of the Old Testament, especially for Jews, are the first five books, called 'the books of Moses' (because God gave Moses the Ten Commandments on tablets of stone) or the 'Torah' or the 'Pentateuch'. Besides the account of the beginning of the world, they also include books of laws, notably Leviticus, which gives instructions on how the tribe should govern its day-to-day life. These cover every aspect of living, for example how to handle sickness in the tribe, the division of property between family members, and rules concerning marriage. We also see God choosing 'Israel' to be his people, and Abraham to be the Father of the nation. The covenant is then re-made with each successive leader or patriarch: Noah, Abram, Isaac, Jacob, Joseph and Moses.

When the Jews move to Egypt to escape famine and become oppressed by the Egyptians as slaves, God helps Moses to rescue his people and lead them through the Red (or possibly 'Reed') Sea. He gives them food and water in the desert, and guides them for 40 years until they come to the Promised Land in Canaan. This part of their history is still remembered each year at the Passover meal. During the meal the youngest person present recites the meaning of the escape from Egypt and their time in the desert, saying:

> We were Pharaoh's slaves in Egypt, and the Lord our God brought us forth with a mighty hand and an outstretched arm. And if the Holy One, Blessed be He, had not brought our forefathers forth from Egypt, then we, our children, and our children's children would still be slaves in Egypt. So, even though all of us were wise, all of us full of understanding . . . we should still be under the commandments to tell the story of the departure from Egypt. And the more one tells the story of the departure from Egypt, the more praiseworthy He is.

(John Drane, Introducing the
Old Testament, Oxford, Lion, 2000, p. 50)

The entrance into Canaan, or the 'Promised Land', was not to be quite what they expected. First they had to remove the inhabitants already settled there! God gave Moses laws for his people, that included the Ten Commandments, but Moses himself was not to enter the Promised Land with his people. That task was to be left to his successor, Joshua.

The Ten Commandments: Exodus 20

I am the Lord your God, who brought you out of the land of Egypt out of the house of slavery.

- You shall have no other God.
- You shall not make for yourself an idol.
- Do not make wrongful use of the name of the Lord your God.
- Observe the Sabbath day.
- Honour your father and mother.
- You shall not murder.
- You shall not commit adultery.
- Neither shall you steal.
- Neither shall you bear false witness.
- Neither shall you covet your neighbour's wife, house . . .

Poetry

One of the greatest books in the Bible is the book of Psalms. The Hebrew title means 'songs of praise', for these poems are intended to be sung. They cover a multitude of subjects: sorrow at committing sin, delight in worshipping God, trust that God will save his people from a particular evil, and walking in the dark by the light of faith. The style is down-to-earth and direct. The individuals praise and worship God, but they also shout and complain to him. The images used are those of everyday life in the fields, or on the water or in the Temple. Perhaps because of their directness they have always found favour with Christians. Psalms like Psalm 23 (see p. 60) and Psalm 46 have become the inspiration to dozens of song-writers.

The Psalms, often known as the 'hymn book of the Second Temple', were certainly used in the Temple after the Jews returned from the exile in Babylon, but many of the 150 psalms were written at a much earlier date. Although they are often ascribed to King

Psalms and their counterparts, hymns
Psalm 23

The Lord is my shepherd, I shall not want.
He makes me lie down in green pastures;
He leads me beside still waters;
He restores my soul.

Hymn: 'The Lord's my shepherd'
(Francis Rous (1579–1659); Melody: Crimond)

The Lord's my shepherd, I'll not want;
He makes me down to lie
in pastures green; He leadeth me
the quiet waters by.

Psalm 148

Praise the Lord!
Praise the Lord from the heavens;
praise him in the heights!
Praise him, all his angels;
praise him, all his host!

Praise him, sun and moon;
praise him, all you shining stars!
Praise him, you highest heavens,
and you waters above the heavens!

Hymn: 'Praise the Lord, you heavens' (Foundling Hospital
(1796) and E. Osler (1798–1863); Melody: Croatian folk tune)

Praise the Lord, you heavens, adore Him;
praise Him, angels in the height!
sun and moon, rejoice before Him;
praise Him, all you stars and light!
praise the Lord, for He has spoken:
worlds His mighty voice obeyed;
laws, which never shall be broken,
for their guidance He has made.

David, it is difficult to know which might actually have been written by this warrior king.

Not all the poems or songs in the Old Testament are found in the book of Psalms. The book of Lamentations is a collection of five poems that lament the destruction of Jerusalem. The poet is bitter at the way God seems to have abandoned his people and let them be taken off to Babylon, leaving the ruin of Jerusalem abandoned. Other books include poems as part of the work: e.g. Nahum opens with the Creator God shown as bringing the earth into being from chaos.

The Old Testament also contains a number of songs. Miriam, the sister of Aaron and Moses, was a prophetess who led the women of Israel in dance and song after the crossing of the Red Sea (Exodus 15.20–21), while the Song of Deborah in the book of Judges (Judges 5.2–31) is possibly one of the oldest songs in the Bible.

Differing accounts

Over the centuries the books of the Old Testament have been transcribed, copied and sometimes 'improved' – for instance, see Josiah's reforms when the Book of the Law is found by Hilkiah (2 Kings 22—23). We can also see an example of this in the story of the creation of the world in Genesis. Hidden in the text in a section of the Bible that we know so well, it is still possible to see that there are actually two accounts imposed upon one another (see pp. 62 and 63).

If you read the Old Testament cover to cover you will also notice that, as well as stories being imposed upon one another, there are also a number of sections that are repeated. In particular the stories concerning King David are repeated in a later and revised version: 1 Chronicles 10—36 substantially parallels 1 Samuel 31—2 Kings 25.

The Old Testament did not come to its present state until well into the Christian period. In pre-Christian times there was great debate about which books should be included in any officially

Two creation accounts

In the beginning when God created the heavens and the earth, the earth was a formless void and darkness covered the face of the deep, while a wind from God swept over the face of the waters. Then God said, 'Let there be light'; and there was light. And God saw that the light was good; and God separated the light from the darkness. God called the light Day, and the darkness he called Night. And there was evening and there was morning, the first day.

And God said, 'Let there be a dome in the midst of the waters, and let it separate the waters from the waters.' So God made the dome and separated the waters that were under the dome from the waters that were above the dome. And it was so. God called the dome Sky. And there was evening and there was morning, the second day . . .

Then God said, 'Let us make humankind in our image, according to our likeness; and let them have dominion over the fish of the sea . . .'

(Genesis 1.1–8, 26)

recognized canon. Indeed, the Samaritans refused to acknowledge anything other than the Pentateuch for their Scriptures, while in Christian times many communities continued to dispute whether books like Ezekiel and Proverbs should be included in the official canon of the Old Testament. Until the Reformation in England there were still questions about the authenticity of the Apocrypha, and whether or not it should be included in the Bible. The Roman Catholic Church insisted that it should, but most 'reformed' Churches chose not to include it in their Bibles. The

These are the generations of the heavens and the earth when they were created.

In the day that the LORD God made the earth and the heavens, when no plant of the field was yet in the earth and no herb of the field had yet sprung up – for the LORD God had not caused it to rain upon the earth, and there was no one to till the ground; but a stream would rise from the earth, and water the whole face of the ground – then the LORD God formed man from the dust of the ground, and breathed into his nostrils the breath of life; and the man became a living being. And the LORD God planted a garden in Eden, in the east; and there he put the man whom he had formed. Out of the ground the LORD God made every tree that is pleasant to the sight and good for food, the tree of life also in the midst of the garden, and the tree of knowledge of good and evil.

(Genesis 2.4–9)

Church of England kept it for 'edification' and example, rather than for authority.

Through the books of the Old Testament we see that God is with his people from their earliest times, to the establishment of their own kingdom. We see his loving care for them, even when they slip back to worship old gods, or ignore his wishes. We see how the prophets continued to speak out against the people, urging them to return to the Lord whenever they strayed, and gradually we see how these same prophets foresee that God will deliver his people. They begin to look forward to the coming of a Messiah, although that Messiah is pictured in a number of different ways.

Bible work: the Old Testament

Look up these references to get a flavour of the early history of the people of God in the Old Testament:

- God calls Abram: Genesis 12.1–3.
- God makes a covenant with Abram: Genesis 15.18–21.
- God calls Moses: Exodus 3.1–15.
- The exodus from Egypt and the first Passover: Exodus 12—14.
- A chosen people: Deuteronomy 7.1–6.

The New Testament

The books of the New Testament were not collected into their present format until some centuries after the death of Jesus. The four Gospels, Matthew, Mark, Luke and John, give us four 'snapshots' of Jesus, and in particular of the three years before his death with his disciples. The first three Gospels have similarities and are called the 'Synoptic Gospels', because they look at their subject from the same point of view. It is likely that they were written by different people with some material held in common, after the year AD 65.

The four Gospels, as can be seen on p. 65, were written by different people at different times. The exact names of the authors of the Gospels are unknown, but they are usually referred to by their traditional names.

Mark's Gospel, the first to be written, seems to have been

New Testament dates

AD 29–30	The death and resurrection of Jesus.
AD 30–40	The stories concerning Jesus are collected together, initially orally.
AD 50	The letters (that is, the Epistles) are written.
AD 65	Gospel of St Mark, written in Rome apparently for Roman Christians. Papias in AD 140 wrote that Mark was a companion of Peter and that he wrote down all that he could remember.
AD 70	Gospel of St Luke, mentions the destruction of Jerusalem in Luke 21.20, that occurred in AD 70.
AD 85–90	Gospel of St Matthew, which uses most of St Mark's Gospel, plus some sayings in common with St Luke and some of his own material.
AD 90+	Gospel of St John; early tradition connects John's Gospel with Ephesus in Asia Minor, although Alexandria has some claim for the place of origin. It is thought that John's Gospel is dependent on the Synoptic Gospels.

---

produced for Roman converts. It does much to explain Jewish customs. It is also much shorter and more clipped than the other Gospels, yet his stories are commonly more detailed and vivid than some of the other parallel accounts. Mark's Gospel also appears more like a biography of the life of Jesus, even though Mark says it is a Gospel and therefore not a biography.

Luke was perhaps a doctor and a Gentile (a non-Jew). His Gospel is the most inclusive, giving us stories about women and outcasts, stories like the Good Samaritan, and Lazarus and the Rich Man. His Gospel also includes many of our most loved stories: the birth stories involving Mary and her relative Elizabeth, and the 'lost' parables of Chapter 15.

Matthew in his Gospel also gives an account of Jesus' birth, in this case from Joseph's perspective, and tells of the new family's flight to Egypt. Written largely for the Jewish community, this Gospel shows Jesus as a great teacher, and includes many references to the Old Testament Scriptures to prove that Jesus was the long-awaited Messiah.

John's Gospel was written in Greek and was the last to appear, sometime after AD 90. His Gospel is designed to show the glory of Jesus who is the Son of God. As such, Jesus' miracles are 'signs' of not his, but God's glory. They are usually accompanied by comment or dialogue in which their spiritual importance is brought out. John's Gospel stands alone as the most wonderful personal testament to faith in Jesus Christ. It is probably the most loved of the Gospels, with Chapter 14 as one of its highlights.

The writer of Luke's Gospel also wrote the Acts of the Apostles, which is an account of the experiences of the new Church as they learn to live without Jesus, but with the help of the power of the Holy Spirit. Acts tells of the spread of the gospel, the persecution that the new Church faced, and the creation of new Christian communities throughout the Roman Empire. We can cross-reference some of this information with the Epistles or letters of the new Church. Here we see the woes and joys of the new Christians written by their leaders, St Paul, St Peter and others, as they seek to nurture the new churches that have been established around the Roman Empire.

The New Testament closes with the book of Revelation, which is classed with other apocalyptic literature, like the book of Daniel. It was written at a time of great persecution, perhaps in the first century AD during the reign of Domitian, or else slightly later during the reign of Nero. It pulls on Old Testament imagery to create a vision, perhaps to describe what would come out of the horrific conditions in the first century, or else to describe what would happen at the Second Coming of Christ. The book is concerned with inspiring those who are being persecuted and uses symbolic language to describe how God will triumph at the end of time.

Bible work: the New Testament

- Look up some of the stories that only appear in St Luke's Gospel and explore the writer's sympathy with women and with outcasts: remember that a young woman who was pregnant but not married would possibly have been stoned, and that a man who was 'mugged', or another who was working with pigs, would have been outcasts.

  – Elizabeth and Zechariah: Luke 1.5–80.
  – The Good Samaritan: Luke 10.29–37.
  – The Prodigal Son: Luke 15.11–32.

- Read Chapters 14 and 15 of St John's Gospel. Learn a few verses of your favourite passage.

Further work

- Look at both accounts of the Creation in Genesis: 1.1—2.3 and 2.4–23. What are the differences between them? Can you make a decision over which might be earlier and which later?
- Look at the covenant that God makes with Abraham: Genesis 12.1–3. Think about the covenant that you will make with God at your Confirmation. What do you expect from God, and what will you offer him?
- Look at Psalm 139. Choose one or two verses that appeal to you, and copy them out. Find some photographs or pictures to accompany the verses and use them for meditation, or to put on the wall.
- Compare the story of the calling of the first four disciples in the Synoptic Gospels: Matthew 4.18–22, Mark 1.16–20, Luke 5.1–11. What are the differences between the accounts?

- Choose your favourite Gospel, buy a commentary from a Christian bookshop, and start to read, using the commentary to help you understand what you are reading.
- Look at the early story of Saul (who becomes St Paul) from the stoning of Stephen (Acts 7.58—8.3 and 9.1–30). Think about how the disciples might have felt about Paul's conversion. How would you have felt?

Research

- Using a Bible that indicates which parables and miracles appear in which Gospels, list which well-known stories appear only in one of the Gospels. If we only had, say, Mark and Luke, what stories would be missing?
- Look at the birth stories in Matthew and Luke. How much of our Christmas story would be missing if we only had Matthew?
- Look up the website <www.virtualreligion.net/primer> or <www.utoronto.ca/religion/synopsis> and compare texts of, say, 'The Sower' in Matthew, Mark and Luke. What are the differences?

Prayer and reflection

Light a candle, and use an icon or flowers as a focal point for worship. Use the Collect for the Last Sunday after Trinity:

> Blessed Lord,
> who caused all holy Scriptures to be written for our
>   learning:
> help us so to hear them,
> to read, mark, learn and inwardly digest them
> that, through patience, and the comfort of your holy
>   word,
> we may embrace and for ever hold fast
> the hope of everlasting life,

which you have given us in our Saviour Jesus Christ,
who is alive and reigns with you,
in the unity of the Holy Spirit,
one God, now and for ever. Amen.

Reading for worship
- Psalm 119.103–105.

Sing one of these:

- 'Tell me the stories of Jesus'
- 'Open my eyes that I may see'

Close with a prayer for help in understanding the Bible, and for those who find it difficult to read and understand the Scriptures. Pray for those who live in countries where to own and to read a Bible is dangerous.

CHRISTIAN BELIEF

7

Keeping in touch with God: Prayer

Throughout his life Jesus seems to have set aside time to be with his Heavenly Father, God. We can see from the Gospels that throughout the three years of his ministry nothing was carried out without reference to God. At the beginning of his ministry he was driven by the Holy Spirit into the wilderness of the Judean desert. His 40-day fast in the desert reflects the 40 years that the Jews spent in the wilderness. Here, away from the distractions of everyday life, he was tested, as the Bible says, 'by Satan' (Mark 1.13).

Some Christians understand Satan (or the Devil) to be a fallen angel and the personification of all that is evil; others see Satan as a metaphor for evil and for all rebellion against God. Whatever our personal belief about this, we do know that in the solitude of the desert Jesus wrestled with the challenges that were presented to him. Like all humans, Jesus was faced with the temptation of making wrong choices. But as the Son of God he was also faced with a different set of temptations. However, in the solitude of the desert through prayer he made the right choices. Now Jesus was ready to start his ministry.

During his day-to-day life on earth, Jesus showed us the need for prayer, and we can learn a lot by observing how and when Jesus spent time in prayer. He set specific time aside, often going somewhere quiet to start the day with God, or ending a particularly intense time of healing with prayer. He also attended the local synagogue where possible, and the Temple when he happened to be in Jerusalem.

Jesus and prayer

- Jesus prays alone: Mark 1.35, Mark 6.46.
- Pray in secret: Matthew 6.5–6, Mark 1.36–37.
- Jesus gets up early to pray: Mark 1.35.
- How to pray: Matthew 6.7–13.
- Jesus prays all night before choosing his disciples: Luke 6.12–13.
- Jesus prays with his disciples: Luke 9.28–29.
- Need for constant prayer: Luke 18.1–8.
- Jesus prays before his arrest: Matthew 26.36–46.
- Jesus attends the synagogue: Mark 1.21.

Through his example Jesus also taught his followers the need to be with God and to set aside time for him. At the prompting of his disciples, he also taught them how to pray using the words of the Lord's Prayer. The order is one we can use as a pattern for our own prayer:

- *Our Father in heaven*: Jesus teaches us to address God directly and personally, not through intermediaries.
- *Hallowed be your name*: God's holy name is special, and not to be taken in vain. He is to be praised, and praise is to be our first thought when addressing God.
- *Your kingdom come*: we continually pray for God's Kingdom of love and peace to come to completion in our world.
- *Your will be done on earth as it is in heaven*: we pray that God's wishes will be carried out in our own lives and in our world.
- *Give us today our daily bread*: we ask God to provide all his people with food, and we remind ourselves that we too should help those who have no food.
- *Forgive us our sins as we forgive those who sin against us*: we ask God's forgiveness for our sins, and request his help in forgiving those who have hurt us.

- *Lead us not into temptation but deliver us from evil*: we ask God's help not to be tempted, and to keep us safe from any harm.

A final phrase was added later:

- *For the kingdom, the power and the glory are yours now and for ever*. Amen: the prayer ends, as it started, in praise of God.

Bible work

Read the different accounts of the Lord's Prayer in Matthew and Luke:

- Matthew 6.9–13.
- Luke 11.2–4.

What differences are there?

Jesus taught his disciples that God loves us and that he wants to be in a close relationship with us. God knows all about us: he knows our needs, our weaknesses and our strengths. But God wants us to acknowledge that we need him, and to turn to him in the natural way that we turn to someone whom we love. He is to be our Father, an example of the best kind of parental relationship.

Only when we turn to God in this way do we begin to understand what it is God wants in our lives and in the world. As we grow closer to God, only then do we begin to see through his eyes. Looking through God's eyes means we shall see the world in a different light, and then we are more likely to ask for the right kind of help.

Jesus also taught that we should persevere with our prayer. We should not give up. We must keep on asking God for what we need, for he will give his Holy Spirit to those who ask him. He taught his disciples to:

Ask, and it will be given to you; search, and you will find; knock, and the door will be opened for you. For everyone who asks receives, and everyone who searches finds, and for everyone who knocks, the door will be opened.

(Luke 11.9–10)

Jesus also told the Parable of the Widow and the Unjust Judge to encourage his followers to persevere in prayer. We are to pray without ceasing. The judge is an unjust judge, respecting neither God nor man. The widow is poor and vulnerable. She is the opposite in every way to the judge. It is only through her sheer stubbornness that she wears the judge down so that he finally listens to her case. Jesus uses this parable to exhort his followers to follow the example of the widow and to pray without ceasing:

Though I have no fear of God and no respect for anyone, yet because this widow keeps bothering me, I will grant her justice, so that she may not wear me out by continually coming. (Luke 18.4b–5)

We are to persevere with our prayer and continually knock on God's door, rather like the widow. Prayer will not be easy; it is hard work. We should persevere at all costs in asking God for what is needed.

Prayer is . . .

Prayer can be likened to a two-way conversation on a telephone. Imagine making a telephone call to a loved one. There is a lot of information to give – what has happened during the day, what has gone wrong, and what has been successful. Help may be needed, and forgiveness sought. The other person may need to be thanked.

All this is quite normal. It is what we do when we make a phone call to someone we love. But there is one other thing that we always do! We listen to the other person on the phone. It would be a strange conversation if we only spoke and then put the phone down.

However, when we speak to God we often forget to listen to him. Our precious time with God can be used to relate a verbal 'shopping list' of requests.

Just as we hold one-to-one conversations on the phone so we can also hold one-to-one conversations with God in our prayer time. Just as we can engage in a 'conference call' and speak to a number of different people on the phone, so we can also pray with other Christians in church during worship or in a prayer group. Alternatively, silent prayer can be used, particularly on Quiet Days or on retreats. Praying alone or together should be as natural as breathing, though we may want to be slightly circumspect about intimate or confidential details of our life or the lives of others when we pray together in public.

Types of prayer

There are many different kinds of prayer, and Christians need to become accustomed to them. The easiest way of remembering them is to use the abbreviation ACTS. This stands for:

- Adoration;
- Confession;
- Thanksgiving;
- Supplication.

Adoration

There are times in life, particularly in the presence of the natural world, when we feel full of praise and adoration for God. We may want to shout or dance with joy at seeing a beautiful sunset, a mountain covered in heather, or the wild grandeur of the sea. Experiences like these can make us feel full of awe and wonder, so that we naturally turn to God in praise and adoration.

Confession

Often we fail to live up to God's standards, and we need to learn to admit our failures, in the same way that we would confess them to a friend or family member. God is always ready to forgive us when we are honest with ourselves, and with him. We say in the prayer after Communion: 'when we were still far off you met us in your Son and brought us home'. God is already there waiting for us when we confess our sin. Confession can occur in a number of ways. It may be corporate and public in worship, or private in the presence of a priest, or it can occur in the silence of our hearts.

Thanksgiving

We have so much in our lives for which to thank God. We may have a comfortable and warm home, loving family members and good health. Even when things are not perfect there is always something for which to be grateful, and we need to remember to thank God for his generosity to us. The writer of the old chorus 'Count your blessings' knew this:

> Count your blessings,
> Name them one by one,
> Count your blessings,
> See what God has done,
> Count your blessings,
> Name them one by one,
> And it will surprise you
> What the Lord has done.

Supplication

Lastly, we come to intercession: that is, our prayer for other people. We must not assume that, because God knows what is wanted, we should not ask for his help. Jesus taught us that we should ask. In intercession we are putting ourselves in another's shoes, and trying to imagine what it is they need. But intercession should also be the first call to action. We cannot just leave things to God to sort out. Having asked his help we should also be prepared to act, to help bring about change to God's world.

Prayers and prayer styles

Over the centuries many famous Christians have written prayers, and it is worth getting to know their styles and some of their most famous prayers. Look out for prayers by St Augustine, St Teresa and St Francis of Assisi and collect them in a personal prayer book. Use them as part of your normal prayer life.

Discover how to use your imagination when praying. A number of parables and miracles can be used as stimulus for your imagination. Miracles – like the healing of Simon's mother-in-law (Luke 4.38–39), the healing of the paralysed man (Luke 5.17–25) and the healing of the blind beggar (Luke 18.35–43) – and parables – like the Parable of the Sower (Matthew 13.3–8) – can all be used. See 'Further work' for an example of how to use your imagination in prayer.

Use the Bible to enhance your prayer life, or the prayer life of any group. There are many prayers in the Bible, in particular in the Old Testament. Sometimes the text needs changing slightly, e.g. 'The peace of God, which surpasses all understanding, will guard *your* hearts and *your* minds in Christ Jesus' (Philippians 4.7) needs to be changed to *our*. The Psalms are a particularly fruitful place to search for prayers, but so also are the Epistles. For example:

> Give ear to my words, O LORD;
> give heed to my sighing.
> Listen to the sound of my cry,
> My King and my God,
> For to you I pray.
> (Psalm 5.1–2)

> To you, O LORD, I lift up my soul.
> O my God, in you I trust . . .
> (Psalm 25.1–2a)

O give thanks to the LORD, for he is good,
for his steadfast love endures for ever.
O give thanks to the God of gods,
for his steadfast love endures for ever.
O give thanks to the LORD of lords,
for his steadfast love endures for ever.

(Psalm 136.1–3)

May the God of peace, who through the blood of the eternal covenant brought back from the dead our Lord Jesus, that great Shepherd of the sheep, equip you with everything good for doing his will, and may he work in us what is pleasing to him, through Jesus Christ, to whom be glory for ever and ever. Amen. (Hebrews 13.20–21, NIV)

Praise be to the God and Father of our Lord Jesus Christ, who has blessed us in the heavenly realms with every spiritual blessing in Christ. For he chose us in him before the creation of the world to be holy and blameless in his sight.

(Ephesians 1.3–4, NIV)

Prayer triplets are a good way to pray. Agree with two other people to pray together at a certain time or on a certain day. The prayers may be said separately with the group never actually meeting. Agree the subject(s) for prayer, and meet occasionally to review results.

Another style of prayer can be found in Scotland. Celtic prayers have a style all their own, concentrating on nature, on the sea, on mountains and on the sky. Often they use repetition and response to achieve a fresh style. Iona and Lindisfarne islands have both produced modern Celtic-style prayers (see, for example 'God in all' on p. 78).

God in all

In your walking – God
In your talking – God
In your life – God
In your strife – God
In your seeing – God
In your being – God
In your days – God
In your ways – God
In your night – God
In your plight – God
In your reason – God
In every season – God

With God I'm bound
All around
The Trinity
Circle me.
Father
Profound.
Jesus
Confound.
Spirit
Abound.
With God I'm bound
All around.
(David Adam, *Tides and Seasons*,
London, Triangle/SPCK,
1989, p. 20)

Prayer tips

- Prayer needs to be regular and constant.
- Initially pray for just a few minutes each day.
- Find somewhere quiet to pray.
- Get comfortable; you don't have to kneel.
- Keep a prayer diary of who or what you are praying for.
- Don't pray if you are tired – unless you need to fall asleep!
- Write your own prayers, and use them.
- Read a paper or listen to the news. Give thanks for what you discover, and also ask God's help for situations that need his intervention.
- Create your own routine to suit your circumstances, using your own words.
- Pray for your church, your vicar, and your family!

Further work

- Count your blessings – make a list of all the good things in your life. Use the list in your prayers, to thank God.
- Use 'arrow' prayers (quick dart-like prayers often said during daily life, but in the silence of our hearts) whenever quick intercession is needed.
- Read Psalm 46.10a. Repeat the words slowly. Then repeat the words again, and again, each time dropping off the last word or two, as appropriate, ending with 'Be still':

> Be still, and know that I am God!
> Be still, and know that I am
> Be still, and know that I
> Be still, and know that
> Be still, and know
> Be still, and
> Be still!

- Listen to a piece of music or read through a favourite hymn. Use this as an aid to prayer and reflection.
- Create your own prayer book. Take a blank notebook and write out favourite prayers, e.g. prayers by Mother Teresa or Francis of Assisi. Learn some by heart.
- Pray over the day: think back over the day, remembering everything that you have done. Then go back over the day again, pausing at anything that needs to be confessed, or to pray for others, or yourself.
- Use the 'Jesus Prayer'. Say it over and over again in the silence of your heart: 'Lord Jesus Christ, Son of the Living God, have mercy on me, a sinner.'
- Pray using your imagination. To check you have some imagination, try to picture a large fat cat sitting on top of your television! Then clear your mind of this odd image, and imagine you have been born with a withered arm. Look at the arm and see its deformity. Try to use it and notice its limitations. Your friends have decided to take you to see Jesus. What do you feel about this? You come before Jesus, and he touches your arm. What does it feel like? You look down at the arm, and you can move your fingers. How do you feel? Look at the newly healed skin, see how you can stretch the arm above your head . . . ! Close by thanking God for:

  - the way he heals his people;
  - the work of doctors and nurses;
  - all who are sick and who need our prayers.

Research

- Find out about worship and prayer in any of the following communities: Franciscans, Benedictines, Ignatians.

Prayer and reflection

Light a candle, and use an icon or flowers as a focal point for worship. Use one or more of the prayer ideas above. Perhaps start by playing a piece of music, then sit in silence before using your imagination.

Readings for worship

- Psalm 5.1–7.
- John 14.1–6.

Sing one of these:

- 'Father, I place into your hands'
- 'Father, we adore you'
- 'Lord, teach us how to pray aright'
- 'O Lord, hear my prayer'

CHRISTIAN BELIEF

8

God and his people:
The Church and worship

— ◆ —

The Greek word *ekklesia* is translated as 'Church' in the New Testament, but it might more accurately be translated as 'an assembly called together'. The Church is therefore not the building, but the people. It was established by Jesus, who explained the relationship between the Church and himself using an image from nature. He said, 'I am the vine, you are the branches' (John 15.1–8). We are to be like branches of a tree, which cannot grow unless they are firmly attached to the trunk of the tree. We are also to 'remain in him'. One of the ways in which we remain like branches attached to God is to pray. When we pray on our own we grow closer to God, and that is important. But praying with others in the Church helps us build up our relationship with God *and* with each other.

The Church is sometimes called the 'Family of God', and as with any family it is good sometimes to be alone, but it is also good to be together. As the Family of God we are given the 'good news' of Jesus Christ to share with other people. We are born into the church family at our Baptism, and become members along with others who are our brothers and sisters in Christ. However, we can still be selfish. The word 'I' is often too important to us. In the Christian life 'we' should be more important. God's plans are for his world, and for us as part of that world. It is almost impossible to say we belong to a family if we never meet together. So it is almost impossible to say we are Christians if we never meet with God's people in worship. Worship is not an optional extra, it is a necessity for building up the Family of God.

The early Church

In the early days of the Church after Pentecost when the Holy Spirit had come upon the new Christians, they met constantly together for worship. Each day they revelled in the excitement of knowing that Jesus had defeated death, and that he had called them to take the gospel of the good news of Jesus Christ to the world. In the Acts of the Apostles we read that:

> They devoted themselves to the apostles' teaching and fellowship, to the breaking of bread and the prayers . . . Day by day, as they spent much together in the temple, they broke bread at home and ate their food with glad and generous hearts, praising God and having the goodwill of all the people. (Acts 2.42, 46)

We learn that the new Christians supported one another financially, provided for those with no income, and cared for the widows and orphans. As we can see from the Acts of the Apostles, the regular coming together for prayer, worship, study and fellowship was most important. The breaking of bread, which eventually became the Communion service, also helped to nurture the new community, bringing them closer to each other and to God.

Worshipping God

The word 'worship' means 'giving God his worth'. We worship something or someone that we deem to have worth. The early Christians, and the Jews before them, met to offer God praise and thanksgiving. They deemed that God, who had made the world and who sought to care for them, was worthy of their 'worth-ship'. The Psalmists recognized that God who made the world, and who rescued them again and again, was worthy of their adoration and praise.

Sometimes we choose to be quiet in the presence of God. Over the centuries men and women who wanted to live in solitude left the world behind to become hermits, and worshipped in silence. At other times, however, we may wish to sing or dance in praise of God. Worship is not just a cerebral activity, it can be a physical and emotional experience.

The writers of the Psalms recognized the way that we involve all our senses when we worship God:

Make a joyful noise to God, all the earth;
sing the glory of his name;
give to him glorious praise.
                                    (Psalm 66.1–2)

Clap your hands, all you peoples;
shout to God with loud songs of joy.
For the LORD, the Most High, is awesome,
a great king over all the earth.
                                    (Psalm 47.1–2)

I will give thanks to the LORD with my whole heart;
I will tell of all your wonderful deeds.
I will be glad and exult in you;
I will sing praise to your name, O Most High.
                                    (Psalm 9.1–2)

The Church today

Today Christians still meet as did their early forebears, to praise God, to encourage one another, and to build up the Family of God. However, just as families may live in different ways, so different churches today worship God in slightly different ways. They still remain part of the Family of God, but the denominations have found differing ways of expressing their worship of God. There are nearly 1,000 million Christians in the world. The majority belong to the Roman Catholic Church and the Orthodox Church (which can be Coptic, Russian or Greek Orthodox). The Roman Catholic Church, the largest denomination, is led by the Pope based in the Vatican in Rome, with the help of cardinals and bishops throughout the world. Like the Church of England the Roman Catholic Church uses dioceses to divide countries into smaller areas. Each diocese is headed by a bishop.

The 'Nonconformist' or Protestant Churches are composed of many different denominations. Together with the Church of England these broke away from the Roman Catholic Church in the sixteenth and seventeenth centuries. They principally consist of:

- Lutherans;
- Baptists;
- Methodists;
- United Reformed Church;
- Presbyterians;
- Pentecostals.

Over the past few decades a number of different congregations have made covenants (agreements) to join together in ecumenical projects (known as Local Ecumenical Projects or LEPs). So a church congregation might be composed of Methodists, Baptists and Church of England members, working together to carry out mission in a specific place. The intention has been not to create new denominations, but to live and work together as one Church, respecting each other's traditions and learning from one other. As well as this the Church of England and the Methodist Church, as a whole, are seeking to work towards creating a united Church.

The Church of England

The Church of England (or Anglican Church) was established at the Reformation in the sixteenth century and is now a worldwide

Church, having spread alongside colonialism across the world. Despite pressure at the time to become more 'Protestant' (in the reign of Queen Elizabeth I) and by others more 'Catholic' (in the reign of Mary), it remained broad enough to hold within it a variety of shades of opinion. The breadth of churchmanship encompasses almost all of that found in the other denominations. There are congregations as catholic as the Roman Catholic Church, and as evangelical as the Baptist or Pentecostal Church.

Another way of describing the difference in churchmanship is to speak of churches as being 'high' or 'low'. Put simply (and it is only a generalization), the more 'high church' prefer more elaborate services with beautiful vestments and possibly incense. They put a greater emphasis on the sacraments and on the orders of bishop, priest and deacon. The more 'low church' prefer simpler worship, usually put greater emphasis on the Bible rather than the sacraments, and are less concerned with vestments or ritual.

The Church of England has both an Episcopal and a Synodical structure. The Queen as head of state is also the head of the Church of England, and the Archbishop of Canterbury is head of the worldwide Anglican Church.

The Episcopal and Synodical structure of the Church of England

Episcopal structure	Synodical structure
Archbishop of Canterbury	General Synod
Archbishop of York	
Diocesan bishops	Diocesan Synod
Suffragan bishops	
Archdeacons	
Rural or area deans	Deanery Synods
Priests	Parochial Church Councils
Deacons	

Lay people take part in all the Synods, where important matters of faith and order are discussed and where new canons (laws) are made. Important subjects that might radically change the Church are sent from General Synod to deanery or parish level for discussion and voting, before being finally discussed again at General Synod. Some laws are also sent to Parliament for ratification. The checks and balances of being both Episcopal and Synodical keep the Church from being controlled by one particular group.

Every parish in the Church of England is run by an incumbent (a parish priest) and two churchwardens. Together they hold the church assets in trust. They are assisted by the Parochial Church Council. Each church has a Church Electoral Roll, and those living in the parish or attending church regularly may place their name on it, and may attend the Annual Parochial Church Meeting. Only those on the Electoral Roll may stand as members of the Parochial Church Council or Deanery or Diocesan Synod.

Some parishes are linked together in benefices, or teams (with a team rector and team vicars), or groups. Many parish priests now run a number of parishes; the tendency for multi-benefices is growing, and the need for mature lay people to help play their part in helping to run the local church is increasing.

Priests in the Church of England are trained at theological colleges. At ordination they are ordained deacon and wear a stole (their 'badge' of office) diagonally over one shoulder. From their ordination as a deacon they wear a clerical collar, affectionately known as a 'dog collar', and are known as the Reverend . . . As a deacon they may preach, lead worship, baptize and conduct funerals. They may not conduct the Communion service or absolve or give a blessing. At the end of a year they are usually ordained priest, and their stole is placed over both shoulders. They may now conduct Communion and carry out weddings.

Deacons and priests may be full-time stipendiary clergy (i.e. paid) or non-stipendiary (part-time and unpaid). Some dioceses also have locally ordained ministers who are discerned to have a vocation for ministry and who usually remain with the congregation that has discovered them. Because the Church of England is the authorized Church, priests are given the 'cure of souls' by their bishop. This ensures that every part of the country is under the care of a priest and a parish church. It also allows those who live in the parish to marry in the church and those who die to have their funeral service in church.

The Church of England also has a number of authorized lay orders; the largest of these are readers, who conduct worship, and teach and preach. Some dioceses also have lay pastors, lay elders, and evangelists, who help the parish priest care for the people of the parish and conduct worship and mission in the area in which they are licensed.

The church calendar

The Church follows a calendar for worship through the year, and most denominations follow a common calendar. This ensures that readings cover the life and work of Jesus, as well as that of the early Church. Two or three readings are laid down for services, to include a reading from the Old Testament or the Epistles and a reading from the Gospels. Church seasons are identified by the colour of vestments worn by the clergy, as well as the altar frontals in the church (see the box on p. 89). Different customs are also associated with different festivals: for example, in many churches it is the custom to give out palm crosses on Palm Sunday, and at Easter the paschal candle is lit and kept alight during worship until Pentecost.

Prayer books

For most churches in mainstream denominations, worship will have liturgy or order to it. Patterns of worship have been established over the centuries. All worship in Anglican churches must be authorized and follow that laid down in one of the two prayer books, the Book of Common Prayer (1662) or its alternative, *Common Worship* (2000). Exceptions to this can be when bishops authorize material for local use in their diocese. This might be for

---

Church calendar and colours

Events and dates

Advent: beginning of the church year (four Sundays): purple.

Christmas: birth of Jesus, 25 December: gold or white.

Epiphany: coming of the Wise Men, 6 January: gold or white.

Candlemas: Presentation of Christ in the Temple, 2 February: gold or white.

Ash Wednesday: the beginning of Lent, remembering Jesus' fast in the wilderness of Judea: purple or Lenten.

Palm Sunday: Jesus rode through Jerusalem on a donkey: red.

Maundy Thursday: remembers the Last Supper: white or red.

Good Friday: remembers the crucifixion: red.

Holy Saturday: the beginning of the Easter Vigil: gold or white.

Easter Day: celebrates the resurrection: gold or white.

Ascension Day: ascension of Christ to heaven: gold or white.

Pentecost: the disciples received the Holy Spirit: red.

Trinity Sunday: celebrates the Trinity: gold or white.

---

family worship, or for special services. Clergy swear on the Bible to use only worship that is authorized, to uphold church law, and to obey their bishop and the Queen, on coming into a new post. Clergy are also expected to say the morning and evening office (that is Morning and Evening Prayer) each day.

Both the Book of Common Prayer and *Common Worship* contain services for most eventualities: for example, Morning and Evening Prayer, the Psalms, the Communion service, Baptism, weddings, and funerals. Clergy can decide, together with PCCs, which book to use. Most parish churches now use the Communion service from *Common Worship* for their main mid-morning service on a Sunday, although the Book of Common Prayer (BCP) Holy Communion service is often used for an early morning service. BCP Evensong is still popular.

Both prayer books contain information concerning the date of Easter for many years ahead, as well as that regarding different feast or saints' days. They also include the collects (or special prayers) for different Sundays and festivals. It is the custom now to purchase a separate lectionary that gives the readings for different services throughout the year.

Bible work

Read some of the following descriptions of the Church, as described by Jesus and the early members of the Church. Think about your own church: do these descriptions apply?

- Jesus: the Good Shepherd with his sheep: John 10.11–18.
- Jesus: the true vine and its branches: John 15.1–17.
- St Paul: members of a body: 1 Corinthians 12.27–31.
- St Paul: stones in Christ's Temple: Ephesians 2.19–22.

Further work

- Attend worship at another church, choosing one that is very different from your own. Try to be as objective as possible. Note the differences, and discuss these with your Confirmation group. Can you decide whether your church is high or low, or neither?
- Is your name on the Electoral Roll of the church you attend? This would allow you to vote at the annual meeting and to stand for the Parochial Church Council or Deanery Synod should you wish. See how you can have your name added.

- Find out the names of all those who are leaders in your church and who head up any of the work that might occur there: for example, organist, head of the Mothers' Union or any women's group, flower arranger, treasurer, PCC secretary, children's work.
- Have a look at your church vestments, and notice what colours are used for different periods of the church year. What colour is in use at present?
- Look up the wedding service in the Book of Common Prayer and in *Common Worship*. Notice the opening words explaining the purpose of marriage. How do you feel about this?
- Attend your PCC or Deanery Synod to observe.

Research

- Find out about other churches in your area. What other denominations are there?
- Research information on the Anglican diocese that you live in. What are the names of your diocesan bishop and suffragan (or assistant) bishop(s)? What area does the diocese cover? What deanery do you live in, and who is your area or rural dean?

Prayer and reflection

Light a candle, and use an icon or flowers as a focal point for worship. Write out the names of your parish priest (or members of the ministry team) and the churchwardens, and pray for them.

> Almighty and everlasting God,
> by whose Spirit the whole body of the Church
> is governed and sanctified:
> hear our prayer which we offer for all your faithful people,
> that in their vocation and ministry
> they may serve you in holiness and truth
> to the glory of your name;
> through our Lord and Saviour Jesus Christ. Amen.
>
> (*Common Worship*, Ember Days)

Readings for worship
- Acts 2.41–42.
- Acts 4.33–35.

Sing either of these:

- 'Bind us together, Lord'
- 'I will enter his gates with thanksgiving'

Part 3

THE FUTURE

THE FUTURE

9

Committing to God: Confirmation

————◆◆◆————

Before looking at Confirmation it is necessary to review Baptism. At our Baptism we become a part of God's family the Church, whatever our age, whether child or adult. We join with all those who have chosen to answer God's call to become his people, and through the power of the Holy Spirit we begin the first tentative steps on our spiritual journey.

Baptism for an adult

As adults we are not expected to abide by promises made for us by other people. We can only be held accountable for those promises that we make or break ourselves. So the Church does not expect us to abide by promises made on our behalf by our parents and godparents when we were children. Adults who have not been baptized will usually be baptized within the Confirmation service itself. Here they will make their own response to God!

When a child is baptized (see Chapter 2) the parents and godparents make promises on his or her behalf. It is these same promises that are taken by an adult who has not been baptized. Those coming for Baptism as an adult promise to reject evil and to turn away from sin to live in the light of Christ. The images conjure up a person physically turning his back on all that is unworthy in his life. An old Baptism video, used by clergy with parents of children who come for Baptism, pictures this most vividly. A boy stands before a lighted doorway, with the darkness of the winter's evening at his back. The person in the doorway invites him into the warmth and light of the room beyond. At Baptism we turn with gratitude towards Jesus, who is the 'Light of the world'. Against his goodness, everything else seems dark and unwelcoming.

As well as rejecting evil and turning to Christ, adults who come for Baptism also promise to turn to Christ, as their Saviour and Lord and as the way, the truth and the life. They acknowledge that Jesus has saved them from death, through his death and resurrection, and that he is their sovereign Lord and King. Only through him can they hope to find the way back to God, and to eternal life.

Finally, signed with the sign of the cross and washed clean by the water of Baptism, whether this is sprinkled upon their forehead or through total immersion, they are raised physically and symbolically to a new life. When Baptism and Confirmation both come in the same service, then Confirmation occurs as a 'seal' or 'confirming' of the promises made at the Baptism, even if this has been in the same service.

But only when we are ready will our parish priest steer us towards Confirmation. Often this takes time, after we have wrestled with the challenges of the Christian faith. The turning point comes when we acknowledge that we need God's help. At that point perhaps we seek out another Christian or our parish priest, who guides us towards the Confirmation group. Here we may spend some weeks or months with others, slowly learning more about our faith. We may also spend some time away on retreat.

Even then it is best to wait until we are truly ready for Confirmation, for with Confirmation comes commitment. The Confirmation service is the first day of the rest of our life within the Church. Sometimes this service can be considered by teenagers to be a rite of passage. As such, they see it as the end of childhood and rarely go to church again. For adults, though, it is a new phase of their acceptance by God, and brings with it a deeper level of commitment to God and to the Church.

Confirmation

At Confirmation candidates declare their personal commitment to Christ as responsible adults, and make repentance of their sins before the congregation. They will come before God, as washed of all that would make them unworthy. Initially, the bishop, representing the universal Church, asks them two questions:

- Have you been baptized in the name of the Father, and of the Son, and of the Holy Spirit?
- Are you ready with your own mouth and from your own heart to affirm your faith in Jesus Christ?

The congregation are then asked if they will welcome the candidates and uphold them in their life in Christ. They answer, 'With the help of God, we will.' The congregation of the local church can do much to help new Christians settle into their new life if they will, and should joyfully welcome those whom God is adding to their number.

The bishop reminds the candidates:

- In baptism, God calls us out of darkness into his marvellous light. To follow Christ means dying to sin and rising to new life with him.

Throughout the Baptism service there are images (see Chapter 2) of death and of new life. Those who come to Baptism are to reject or be buried to their past. In the waters of Baptism they are to die to the wrong choices they have made in the past, and be born to a new life with Christ. The symbols of light and water are both used extensively, as we can see from the blessing of the person to be baptized. The priest says:

May Almighty God deliver you from the powers of
    darkness,

restore in you the image of his glory,
and lead you in the light and obedience of Christ.

So, having reminded the candidates of what happened at their Baptism, the bishop then asks six questions:

- Do you reject the devil and all rebellion against God?
- Do you renounce the deceit and corruption of evil?
- Do you repent of the sins that separate us from God and neighbour?
- Do you turn to Christ as Saviour?
- Do you submit to Christ as Lord?
- Do you come to Christ, the way, the truth and the life?

These are challenging questions, and not ones to which we should acquiesce lightly. Turning away from the devil (from all that is opposed to God), from corruption (from all that ruins our relationship with God) and from our sins (from all that results from our estrangement from God) is no easy option. Our saying 'yes' does not necessarily make it happen! It will require great commitment and strength if we are to keep to our promises. However, we are not alone, for God is there to help us, and the candidates affirm that with God's help they will keep the promises.

At this point in the Confirmation service the congregation join in. Together with the candidates they affirm the faith of the whole Church, in the words of the Apostles' Creed (see Chapter 3). If the candidates desire, they may now also make their testimony – that is, they may share with the congregation how God has been at work in their lives up to the present time, and speak about the changes that he has made in their lives.

At the moment of Confirmation the bishop stretches out his hands over the candidates and prays that they will be given the sevenfold gifts of the Holy Spirit (see Chapter 5) before addressing each candidate individually, saying:

- (*Name*) God has called you by name and made you his own.

He then places his hands on the head of each candidate and prays:

- Confirm, O Lord, your servant with your Holy Spirit. Amen.

The candidate's response is 'Amen' (or 'so be it'), signifying his or her agreement with what has been said.

The bishop may choose to anoint the candidates with the fragrant oil of chrism (that is, mixed with various spices). The oil is a sign (see Chapter 2) and seal of the Holy Spirit that gives the newly confirmed Christians the power to fulfil their calling as Christians. If oil is used the bishop anoints them, saying, 'Receive the seal of the Spirit.'

The new life

Having rejected evil, sworn their personal allegiance to Christ and declared their trust in God before the whole congregation, the newly confirmed Christians now look to the future as full and active members of the Church, strengthened in their Christian life by the power of the Holy Spirit.

At this point they and the congregation may receive Holy Communion. Sometimes, perhaps because of the numbers of those involved, and especially if Confirmation is held in the cathedral, the candidates' first Communion may be taken back in their parish church on another day.

In many Confirmation services an optional element is now included. This shifts the mood towards evangelism and mission. As we have seen in Chapter 1, Christians are called by God to do a task. So the whole congregation is reminded of their commission as Christians, to:

- worship and serve God;
- continue in the apostles' teaching and fellowship, in the breaking of bread, and in the prayers;
- persevere in resisting evil, and whenever they fall into sin, to repent and return to the Lord;

- proclaim by word and example the good news of God in Christ;
- seek and serve Christ in all people, loving their neighbour as themselves;
- acknowledge Christ's authority over human society, by prayer for the world and its leaders, by defending the weak, and by seeking peace and justice.

The people of God are called, as a Church, to carry out Jesus' commission to the world. We cannot sit back and do nothing, for we are God's eyes, hands, feet and mouth. Our task is to worship, to teach, to resist evil, to proclaim the good news, to serve Christ by helping others, to pray for others, and to seek justice and peace. It is no small thing to be a Christian!

Post Confirmation

Finally, as a full member of the body of Christ, the newly confirmed Christians will want to make changes to their lives, as we shall see in Chapters 10 and 11. They should ensure that they receive Communion regularly to sustain them for the ongoing journey of commitment as a Christian. They should also begin, if circumstances allow, to give to the Church financially on a regular basis, and will need to speak to the church treasurer or covenant organizer. Even a small amount of money, given regularly and gift-aided if possible, will make a difference to the work that the Church is able to do.

Now is the time, if it has not happened earlier, for the new Christians to make sure that their names go on to the Church Electoral Roll. This is usually carried out in the spring, and will enable them to attend the Annual General Meeting in April and to ask questions, if they wish. At some time in the future they might also wish to stand as a member of the Parochial Church Council or Deanery Synod.

This is also the time to look at what specific task God might be calling the new Christians to do within the congregation of the

Church. As we have seen, God does not wait for us to become trained before he begins to use us. Explore with your local parish priest what work might be appropriate. Every church has a need for workers, and many jobs will need to be done. Among them may be:

- reading the lessons;
- flower arranging;
- leading the intercessions;
- church cleaning;
- typing;
- making refreshments;
- singing in the choir;
- serving at the altar;
- helping with Junior Church.

Bible work

- Read the Great Commission that Jesus gave to his disciples: Matthew 28.18–20. Remind yourself of why you have been called to be confirmed.
- Read Philippians 4.4–7. If you have concerns about anything, including your Confirmation, offer those concerns to God in prayer.

Further work

- If you were baptized as a child, discover what presents you were given. Get someone in the family to tell you about your Baptism, and your Baptism day. Who was present, and exactly what happened?
- Go on retreat for a weekend or for a couple of days, to a local retreat centre. Spend time in meditation thinking about your Confirmation.

- Consider the people in your life. If you are to 'seek and serve Christ in all people', name those in your heart who cause you difficulties. Confess your fault in this poor relationship.
- If the Confirmation is the first day of the rest of your life, how are you intending to live the rest of your life as a Christian? What changes do you intend to make?
- In the Confirmation service you have pledged to 'reject evil'. Think about your life. What is not right in that life? Pray for the help of the Holy Spirit to reject all that is wrong.
- How might you work to help bring justice and peace to the world? What small steps can you take?
- Read Galatians 5.16–25. What 'fruits of the Spirit' have you been given?

Research

- Find out how the early Church admitted new Christians into the Church.
- Find out how the Baptist Church admits adults into full membership of the Church.

Prayer and reflection

Light a candle, and use an icon or flowers as a focal point for worship. Use one of the prayers, on p. 103, from the Confirmation service.

Readings for worship
- Ezekiel 36.25a, 26–28; or
- Ezekiel 37.1–10.

Heavenly Father,
by the power of your Holy Spirit
you give to your faithful people new life in the water of
    baptism.
Guide and strengthen us by the same Spirit,
that we who are born again may serve you in faith and
    love,
and grow into the full stature of your Son, Jesus Christ,
who is alive and reigns with you in the unity of the Holy
    Spirit
now and for ever. Amen.

God of mercy,
by whose grace alone we are accepted
and equipped for your service:
stir up in us the gifts of your Holy Spirit
and make us worthy of our calling;
that we may bring forth the fruit of the Spirit
in love and joy and peace;
through Jesus Christ our Lord. Amen.

Keep, O Lord, your Church, with your perpetual mercy;
and, because without you our human frailty cannot but
    fall,
keep us ever by your help from all things hurtful,
and lead us to all things profitable to our salvation;
through Jesus Christ our Lord. Amen.

Sing one of these:

- 'Come, Holy Spirit'
- 'Amazing grace'

THE FUTURE

10

Growing and belonging: Holy Communion

———◆◆◆———

In our daily life one of the main ways that we express fellowship with people is to invite them to join us for a meal. We meet family members to have lunch together. We go out together with friends in the evening, to enjoy a meal. At festival times, like Christmas or Easter, we get together with relatives to celebrate over a meal. At sad times, like a funeral, we hold a wake, with food. At joyful times, like a wedding, we sit down for a meal. Eating, drinking and being together are normal ways of expressing ourselves as humans.

The Last Supper

In our Christian life it is just the same. One of the most ordinary things we do is to eat a meal together. Jesus spent three years with his disciples: he ate meals with those who were notionally his enemies, like Simon the Pharisee; with his disciples; and with their families, as at the house of Simon's mother-in-law. One of his last activities with his disciples before being arrested in the Garden of Gethsemane was his celebration of the Passover with his friends in an upper room. At this Last Supper they remembered, as they did each year, the time that God had rescued his people, the Jews, from slavery in Egypt. Every detail of the Passover meal is laid down in Exodus 12, and each of them would have celebrated the Passover at home since their childhood. But this time, Jesus made changes to the traditional order.

We can see from all four Gospels that Jesus prepared carefully for his last supper with the disciples. Matthew, for example, says:

> On the first day of Unleavened Bread the disciples came to Jesus, saying, 'Where do you want us to make the preparations for you to eat the Passover?' He said, 'Go into the city to a certain man, and say to him, "The Teacher says, My time is near; I will keep the Passover at your house with my disciples."'
>
> (Matthew 26.17–18)

However, things did not quite follow the pattern for the evening that the disciples would have expected. The normal order of the Passover meal is as follows:

- a prayer of thanksgiving by the leader (or father of a family), and the drinking of a cup of diluted wine;
- the eating of the bitter herbs, to remember the bitterness of their forebears as slaves in Egypt;
- the youngest member asking, 'Why is this night distinguished from all other nights?' and the leader replying by telling the story of the exodus from Egypt;
- the singing of Psalms 113 and 114, and the washing of hands; the drinking of the second cup of wine;
- the eating of the lamb with unleavened bread to commemorate the events of the first Passover;
- the eating of the rest of the meal, and the drinking of the third cup of wine;
- the singing of Psalms 115 to 118; the drinking of the fourth cup of wine.

But if we look at the order of the meal, as described by Luke, for instance, we get this:

- Jesus speaks to his disciples to say that this is to be the last Passover he will eat with them.
- He then eats the Passover meal with the disciples.
- At the end of the meal Jesus then substitutes the 'Lord's Supper'.

While all the men are eating the remains of the meal, Jesus takes some bread, gives thanks and breaks it, before giving it to all those present. 'This is my body, which is given for you. Do this in remembrance of me' (Luke 22.19b). Then he takes one of the cups and does the same thing. 'This cup that is poured out for you is the new covenant in my blood' (Luke 22.20). As the lamb was sacrificed to free the Jews from Egypt, so Jesus will be sacrificed to free all humankind.

The new Church, when it established itself, was to remember the changes made to the Passover meal, and they were to carry out Jesus' commands to hold a meal in remembrance of him.

Different names: same service

Throughout the last 2,000 years the meal that we have held 'in remembrance' of Jesus has had a number of different names. Each carries with it a slightly different emphasis.

- *The Mass*: this name is used by the Roman Catholic Church and comes from the closing words of the old Roman service, *Ite missa est*, which means: go out into the world and do likewise.
- *The Lord's Supper*: used by many Nonconformist Churches because it signifies it was introduced by Jesus, and ensures it is distinguished from any other supper.
- *The Liturgy*: used by the Orthodox Church, presumably to reflect the shape of the service.
- *The Eucharist*: often used by Anglicans, and meaning 'thanksgiving'. It takes its name from the 'thanksgiving' prayer over the bread and wine that sets aside these elements, making them holy.
- *Holy Communion*: also used by Anglicans, emphasizing as it does that we celebrate a holy meal in fellowship with one another.

Although the service of Holy Communion can be taken from either the Book of Common Prayer or *Common Worship*, the variations can still be great. A service held in a tiny chapel or in a house group will be different from that held in a cathedral. In the same way that a meal with friends will be different in one country from another, even if the menu is the same, so Holy Communion will alter according to the country and the place where it is held. Some churches prefer to use wafers and others bread for Communion, some celebrate the meal wearing elaborate vestments with incense and ritual, and others prefer things much simpler. Some churches will use prayer books or home-produced booklets and yet others modern computerized equipment. Some will sing choruses and other will listen to the service sung by a robed choir.

The Communion service as a sacrament

The Communion service is one of seven 'sacraments' or symbolic acts that point to God. The traditional definition is: 'A sacrament is an outward sign of an inward grace' (St Augustine). Sacraments are actions that renew and reconcile the individual and the Church to God. As such they have an outward, visible part (i.e. the action) and an inward, invisible part (the gift of the Holy Spirit that is given to strengthen us).

The seven sacraments:

- Baptism;
- Confirmation;
- The Eucharist;
- Marriage;
- Confession;
- Ordination;
- Anointing the sick.

We sometimes find it hard to put feelings into words. It can be easier to demonstrate through action. Think of the way that we shake hands with someone who is extremely important to us, or give them a kiss of welcome. Often it can be easier to do this than to say something that reflects how we feel! So in the Communion service, at the very heart of our worship in the Church, we eat a sacramental meal. Bread and wine are consumed, we are filled with the Holy Spirit, and we are strengthened for our onward journey of faith.

Although the Communion service is a sacramental meal, if we compare the shape of the service with an ordinary meal held at home we can see how the action compares:

The order of the meal	
President welcomes	Host welcomes the guests.
Readings	Host and guests hear the stories of the past and of friends.
Sermon	We learn something based on what we have heard.
Intercessions	We think about those absent or who have problems.
Peace	We celebrate our togetherness.
Offertory	Food and wine are brought to the table.
Thanksgiving	We give thanks for the meal.
Communion	We eat and drink.
Sending out	We say farewell.

Confessing our sin

The one element not mentioned above is the Confession. It is necessary to work at keeping a relationship healthy. When we fall out with friends it is essential, if the relationship is to continue, to find a way of repairing things. Saying 'sorry' can be difficult, but unless we are prepared to admit our mistakes and ask forgiveness from our friends, we can put that relationship at risk. It can help if we try to imagine ourselves in the position of the other person. How would we feel if someone hurt us?

We also need to work at keeping our relationship healthy with God. When we make mistakes, whether deliberately or not, we need to say 'sorry' to God. At the start of the Communion service we acknowledge this need to be reunited with God by saying the Prayer of Preparation, to help prepare us to receive Communion:

> Almighty God,
> to whom all hearts are open,
> all desires known,
> and from whom no secrets are hidden:
> cleanse the thoughts of our hearts
> by the inspiration of your Holy Spirit,
> that we may perfectly love you,
> and worthily magnify your holy name;
> through Christ our Lord. Amen.

Later we make confession to God for the sins we have committed, remembering that we have sinned against God and against our neighbour, 'in thought and word and deed, through negligence, through weakness, through our own deliberate fault'. We also remember that sometimes we are completely unaware of our mistakes.

It can be easy just to recite the words of the Confession, without giving thought to exactly what we are confessing. Spending some time before the service to think about what we have done or said, or what we have failed to do, is a good idea. After the Confession the priest then absolves our sin, on behalf of God.

What is happening?

Of course, more is going on, symbolically, than appears on the surface. At the Communion service we also link ourselves to God through Jesus, and through him to the whole heavenly host of the Church in the past, present and future. In the Eucharistic Prayer (the Prayer of Thanksgiving), the bread and wine are made holy, or set apart and blessed. As we eat the bread and drink the wine we imitate what happened at the Last Supper, and at that point heaven and earth are brought close together. What we act out is what we believe, and what we act out reinforces our beliefs. This in turn affects our actions and so our beliefs. This cyclical argument about the actions and beliefs of the Holy Communion service is called, in Latin, *lex orandi, lex credendi*.

Anglicans do not believe that the bread and wine become the body and blood of Christ (transubstantiation) as do members of the Roman Catholic Church. Instead, as we have seen, they receive the bread and wine in 'remembrance' and celebrate the fact that Jesus offered himself for sacrifice (instead of a Passover lamb), singing 'Jesus, Lamb of God, you take away the sins of the world'. This was the supreme act of love, which freed us from sin and restored our relationship with God. In receiving the bread and wine, we are reminded of the new life to which we have been called, and we are sustained for our on-going journey of commitment. At the end of the service we are sent out to continue living out the life that Jesus calls his followers to lead.

Bible work

- Compare the story of the Last Supper in Luke 22.7–20 with the Passover actions in Exodus 12.
- Look up and compare the following accounts of the Last Supper, and make a list of all that happens: Matthew 26.17–30, Mark 14.12–26, Luke 22.7–39.
- Look up 1 Corinthians 11.23–26 and compare the account of the Last Supper to one of the accounts from the Gospels.
- Read John 13.1–30, which has an entirely different account of the Passover. What elements are different from those in the Synoptic Gospels?
- Read Psalm 51. This psalm is said on Ash Wednesday as part of the start of the penitential season of Lent. Learn verse 10.

Further work

- Look at one or more of the sacramental services. Can you decide which are the outward actions and which are the invisible gifts that are being given?
- Attend Holy Communion at another church that is very different from the one you usually attend. Notice the differences.
- Participate in a Communion service. Notice all the work of preparation that is needed for a priest to conduct the Communion service: the preparation of the altar; the placement of wafers or bread and wine; and the placement of the correct vestments and altar cloth.
- Watch all the movements that the priest makes at the Eucharist. Notice the work of a server if you have one in your church.

Research

- Find out about 'transubstantiation'. What exactly does it mean?
- Find out more about *lex orandi, lex credendi.*

Prayer and reflection

Take a bread roll, then put a little wine into a wine glass. Add water. Light a candle. Spend some time in reflection. Think about the symbol of bread as Christ's body, and wine as Christ's blood – given for us on the cross.

Reading for worship
- Read 1 Corinthians 11.23–26.

Sing either of these:

- 'I am the bread of life'
- 'Let us break bread together'

Close by saying the words of the prayer used after Communion in *Common Worship*:

> Father of all,
> we give you thanks and praise,
> that when we were still far off
> you met us in your Son and brought us home.
> Dying and living, he declared your love,
> gave us grace, and opened the gate of glory.
> May we who share Christ's body live his risen life;
> we who drink his cup bring life to others;
> we whom the Spirit lights give light to the world.
> Keep us firm in the hope you have set before us,
> so we and all your children shall be free,
> and the whole earth live to praise your name;
> through Christ our Lord. Amen.

THE FUTURE

11

Living as a Christian

———•◆•———

At the Confirmation service the bishop charges the newly confirmed Christians with a Commission, rather in the way that Jesus gave his disciples the Great Commission:

> All authority in heaven and on earth has been given to me.
> Go therefore and make disciples of all nations, baptizing them
> in the name of the Father and of the Son and of the Holy
> Spirit, and teaching them to obey everything that I have com-
> manded you. And remember, I am with you always, to the
> end of the age.   (Matthew 28.18–20)

Just as Jesus charged his disciples to take the gospel to the world, so at Confirmation the bishop charges those who are newly confirmed to live a new life. Their old life has been left behind. They have been born again and are now to start this new life as Christians who are sent out to make a difference in the world in which they live.

The bishop, representing the whole Church, issues the charge as a series of questions. These are to be our priorities, if you like, in the coming years.

First priority

Bishop: Those who are baptized are called to worship
          and serve God.

> Will you continue in the apostles' teaching and
> fellowship,
> in the breaking of bread, and in the prayers?

Our first priority is to worship God. It should be our joy to attend
Holy Communion each Sunday: to praise God, to confess our sin,
to worship with others in the household of faith, to reunite ourselves with the living God, and to leave ready to serve him by continuing his work in the world. Worship should never be boring,
or a waste of time. Corporate worship should be the highlight of
our week, and something that we look forward to attending. If we
do not feel like this, then we must ask ourselves whether we are
putting enough into worship.

Good worship is not just the province of those who lead, it is
also the responsibility of those who attend the service. Worship is
a corporate activity of priest and people, which is one of the reasons why in most Anglican churches the priest and people now
face one another. The best worship will ensure that the whole congregation is involved in the service. It may be led by a priest or
reader, but there will be lay people conducting the intercessions,
reading the lessons and bringing up the bread and wine. It is also
the responsibility of the laity to contemplate their confessions before
the service, to pray for those conducting worship, and if possible
to look at the readings. Some will also be able to help by singing
in the choir, playing the organ or serving at the altar. Whatever
their role, lay people and worship leaders are both responsible for
producing worship of a high standard. For God, nothing but per-
fection is acceptable.

As well as attending worship and receiving Holy Communion,
Christians are called to build up the fellowship of the Body of Christ,
to encourage others in their faith, and to continue 'in the apostles' teaching'. They are to continue learning about their faith, and
putting into practice all that they have been taught during their
time of preparation for their Confirmation. The Confirmation class
is the beginning of a lifetime of learning, and the members of the
group have probably only begun to learn about God. As such, those

who have just been confirmed should continue their learning in a home group or study group.

The bishop's charge includes the reminder that we should 'continue in the prayers'. This means we need to establish a practical and sensible prayer life, that adapts as we grow. Resorting to prayer only when we are desperate is not sufficient. We need to create a prayer pattern and learn to pray with others for our new life to be sustained.

Second priority

Bishop: Will you persevere in resisting evil,
            and, whenever you fall into sin, repent and
                return to the Lord?
            Will you proclaim by word and example
            the good news of God in Christ?

Having promised to live as a Christian, the newly confirmed person must quickly acknowledge that this is not going to be an easy life. It is all too easy to fall into sin by being selfish and trying to 'go it alone'. Despite the best of intentions, we make mistakes and fall away from the true path. We forget to pray and ask for help; we forget to measure our behaviour against that of Jesus. Sometimes we even stop attending worship! Essentially we are attracted by the things of the world to the extent that this can deflect us from pursuing the path that God would have us take.

This is inherently human, and we should not berate ourselves too much. If it were so simple to resist temptation, God would not have had to send his Son to rescue us. The secret is to listen to our conscience, to see clearly what it is that we have done, and to repent of our thoughts, our actions and our deeds. We need to attend worship regularly in order to confess our sins and to put ourselves in a right relationship with God once more. Jesus taught us that God does forgive us when we repent. In the Parable of the Lost Son, when the son has descended to utter degradation, he decides to return home:

So he set off and went to his father. But while he was still far off, his father saw him and was filled with compassion; he ran and put his arms around him and kissed him. Then the son said to him, 'Father, I have sinned against heaven and before you; I am no longer worthy to be called your son.' But the father said to his slaves, 'Quickly, bring out a robe – the best one . . . for this son of mine was dead and is alive again; he was lost and is found!' (Luke 15.20–24)

The son finally makes a decision to return home and ask forgiveness of his father, only to discover that his father has already come out to meet him ready to forgive him. We must remember that in confessing our sin and asking to be forgiven, we must forgive others. One sign of a Christian is the ability to forgive others. We may not be able to forget, and we may not condone another's action, but we should always, with God's help, be able to forgive them.

At the Confirmation service the bishop charges the candidates to proclaim the good news of Jesus Christ. We are to be missionaries from day one, taking the news of what God has done for us to others. The newly confirmed Christian will therefore need to consider what gifts and talents he or she will offer to the Church and its mission. After all, the new Christian does not have to work alone. Depending upon the size and needs of the congregation different tasks will need to be done. A willing worker is always welcome, but it will be necessary to find the right niche. St Paul recognizes that not everyone can be a teacher or a preacher.

Now you are the body of Christ and individually members of it. And God has appointed in the church first apostles, second prophets, third teachers; then deeds of power, then gifts of healing, forms of assistance, forms of leadership . . . Are all apostles? Are all prophets? . . . Do all possess gifts of healing?
(1 Corinthians 12.27–30)

116

The apostle reminds us that we are to hone our gifts in the service of God, for these gifts are not given to us for our own use, but for God's use. We are called by God to do a task. The Epistle of James says: 'What good is it, my brothers and sisters, if you say you have faith but do not have works? Can faith save you? . . . faith by itself, if it has no works, is dead' (James 2.14–17).

Third priority

Bishop: Will you seek and serve Christ in all people,
loving your neighbour as yourself?
Will you acknowledge Christ's authority over
human society,
by prayer for the world and its leaders,
by defending the weak, and by seeking peace and
justice?

The way that we live and work with other people should reflect our belief that we are called to 'seek and serve Christ in all people'. Jesus taught his disciples in the Parable of the Sheep and the Goats (Matthew 25.31–46) that when we seek to help anyone, when we tend the sick or visit the prisoner, then we are serving Christ. He said, 'just as you did it to one of the least of these who are members of my family, you did it to me' (Matthew 25.40). We are called to love all people, and to care for them as we do for ourselves. So we should seek to bring peace and reconciliation to the Church and our community. We are to be God's eyes, his ears, his hands and his feet; we are his agents of action.

As Christians we are also called to acknowledge that Christ is at work in the world, in our human institutions. As such we are to pray for our leaders, and for their actions. God's plans can be carried out through secular institutions in the same way that they can through the Church. We cannot and should not limit God's work! Indeed, we may also feel called to work for the community by becoming an elected member of our local council. Many

Christians have also lived out their calling by working for their country as a Member of Parliament.

Our new life is also to be one of concern for our world and its peoples. We should be concerned with issues like justice, peace and equality. Christians can and should even out the inequalities in our world. We can help to change the world in small ways, through supporting Fair Trade, or writing letters to Amnesty International on behalf of those who have been jailed unfairly, and we can get involved with local community issues.

Our life is to be one of small steps forward. As we grow closer to God, slowly fashioning our life on that of his Son, we shall grow into the kind of person he would have us be.

Bible work

- Read Matthew 25.31–46. Do you find anything surprising about this parable?
- Read Matthew 25.14–30. Does this parable seem fair? What does Jesus mean?
- Read Matthew 13.1–9, 18–23. Which category do you think you fit into?

Further work

- Think about your income. How much can you set aside for the work of the Church? Think about the money you spend each week on things like bread and milk, or a newspaper, or a treat for yourself. Can you give more than this to God? Can it be gift-aided? Speak to your priest or treasurer about giving regularly.
- Decide which gifts you possess and see what the church might require, and then offer to help.
- Join a regular Bible study or home group. Alternatively, buy some Bible-reading notes to help understand the Bible. Keep reading!

- Start the habit of reviewing your week and making a list of things to confess when you attend worship.
- Start the habit of looking up the readings before the Sunday service, and giving some thought to them. It will make the sermon more helpful!

Research

- Find out about the work of Traidcraft and how it helps producers in poorer countries to sell their products at a fairer price across the world.
- Find out about motions coming before General Synod concerning our world or issues connected with peace. Read the reports that are produced.
- Find out about the period of Rogation in the Church's calendar.

Prayer and reflection

Light a candle, and use flowers or something from the natural world as a focal point for worship. Spend some time thinking about what it is you wish to confess, and then ask God's forgiveness. Use the Collect for Social Justice and Responsibility:

> Eternal God,
> in whose perfect realm
> no sword is drawn but the sword of righteousness,
> and no strength known but the strength of love:
> so guide and inspire the work of those who seek your
>   kingdom
> that all your people may find their security
> in that love which casts out fear
> and in the fellowship revealed to us
> in Jesus Christ our Saviour. Amen.

Readings for worship
- Matthew 18.21–22.
- Luke 15.11–32.

Sing one of these:

- 'Go tell it on the mountain'
- 'He's got the whole world'
- 'We are marching'

Close by saying these words from the Book of Common Prayer:

> The love of the Lord Jesus
> draw *us* to himself,
> the power of the Lord Jesus
> strengthen *us* in his service,
> the joy of the Lord Jesus fill *our* hearts;
> and the blessing of God Almighty,
> the Father, the Son, and the Holy Spirit,
> be among *us* and remain with *us* always. Amen.

Appendix
Suggested books for further reading

————◆◆◆————

Bible study

Drane, John (1999) *Introducing the New Testament* (revised edition), Oxford, Lion.

Drane, John (2000) *Introducing the Old Testament* (second, revised edition), Oxford, Lion.

Drane, John (2001) *The New Lion Encyclopedia of the Bible* (new edition), Oxford, Lion.

Harmer, Eric (2002) *Build Your Own Bible Study: A guide to leading study groups*, London, Bible Reading Fellowship.

Wright, Tom (2004) *Mark for Everyone* (New Testament Guides for Everyone) (second edition), London, SPCK.

God

Vardy, Peter (1999) *The Puzzle of God* (third, revised edition), London, Fount.

Prayer books

Appleton, George (2002) *The Oxford Book of Prayer*, Oxford, Oxford University Press.

Bunch, Josephine (1992) *Prayers for Everyday Use*, Norwich, Canterbury Press.

Kendall, R. T. and Louise (2001) *Great Christian Prayers*, London, Hodder & Stoughton.

Spirituality

Adam, David (1987) *The Cry of the Deer: Meditations on the Hymn of St Patrick*, London, Triangle/SPCK.

Adam, David (1985) *The Edge of Glory: Prayers in the Celtic tradition*, London, Triangle/SPCK.

Kempis, Thomas à (2003) *The Imitation of Christ*, London, Dover Publications.

Mission

Church of England Report (2004) *Mission-shaped Church: Church planting and fresh expressions of Church in a changing context*, London, Church House Publishing.

Legg, Steve (2002) *The A–Z of Evangelism: The ultimate guide to sharing your faith*, London, Hodder & Stoughton.

Glossary

Advent	The start of the Christian year, from the Sunday that is nearest to 30 November until Christmas.
Agnostic	A person who is unsure whether God exists.
Altar	The 'table', usually in a chapel or the east end of the church, which represents the table at which Jesus held his last supper with his disciples.
Amen	The word said at the end of a prayer, meaning 'so be it'.
Angel	God's messenger.
Anglican Communion	The worldwide group of Protestant Churches, led by the Archbishop of Canterbury.
Annunciation	The time when the Angel Gabriel came to Mary to tell her that she would bear God's Son.
Apocrypha	Some books of the Bible not accepted by all Christians, found between the Old and New Testaments.
Apostles	The 12 followers of Jesus.
Aramaic	The language that Jesus spoke.
Archbishop	An archbishop is responsible for a number of dioceses. The Church of England has two archbishops, the Archbishop of York and the senior member of the clergy, the Archbishop of Canterbury.
Ascension	Jesus goes back to heaven, 40 days after his resurrection.
Ash Wednesday	The day that begins Lent, the penitential period of the Church's year that leads up to Easter.

Atheist	A person who does not believe in the existence of God.
Atonement	Jesus died to atone for our sins; to be right.
Aumbry	A small cupboard in church where consecrated bread and wine may be kept.
Baptism	The rite of initiation into the Church for a child or an adult.
Baptistery	The place in the church where Baptisms occur.
Beatitudes	A section of the Sermon on the Mount, given by Jesus, and recorded in St Matthew's Gospel, that begins 'Blessed are the . . .'
Bethlehem	The small town where Jesus was born, not far from Jerusalem.
Bible	The Christian Holy Book, containing the Hebrew Scriptures (Old Testament), the New Testament (including the Gospels), and in some cases the Apocrypha.
Bishop	A priest in charge of a diocese, or an assistant bishop (called a suffragan bishop).
Blasphemy	Something spoken against God.
Canaan	Ancient term for the land approximately covered by the area of Israel.
Catholic	Literally means 'universal' Church; sometimes refers to the Roman Catholic Church, or to the Church of England as a 'universal' Church.
Christ	Another name for Jesus.
Christening	Another name for Baptism.
Christian	One who believes in Jesus and follows his teachings.
Christmas	The church festival that celebrates the birth of Jesus.
Church	Either a building used for Christian worship, or the body of Christians.
Church of England	Part of the Anglican Communion, in England. Founded in the sixth century, it broke away

from the Roman Catholic Church during the Reformation and established the monarch as the head of the Church.

Clergy
Another name for those who are given authority to work for the Church. There are three orders: deacon, priest and bishop.

Commandments
God gave Moses these ten laws for the Jewish people.

Communion
The service of Holy Communion 'remembers' the last supper held by Jesus with his disciples, just before his death.

Confirmation
The service at which those who have been baptized re-take their promises to God, and God 'confirms' his gift of the Holy Spirit to them, and his involvement in their lives.

Covenant
A contract or agreement, usually made between an individual and God.

Creed
Statements of what the Church believes. There are three main Creeds: the Apostles' Creed, the Nicene Creed and the Creed of St Athanasius.

Cross
Jesus died on a cross; the most important of Christian symbols.

Crucifix
A cross, with the figure of Jesus upon it.

Day of Judgement
The end of the world, when God will judge all people.

Denomination
A section of the Christian Church, e.g. Methodists, Baptists, Church of England.

Diocese
A section of the Anglican Church or the Roman Catholic Church, run by a bishop.

Disciple
A follower of Jesus.

Easter
The festival of Easter celebrates Jesus' death and resurrection.

Epistles
Letters from members of the early Church, found in the New Testament.

Eucharist
The service of Holy Communion that 'remembers' the last supper held by Jesus

with his disciples, just before his death. (See Communion.) The word 'eucharist' means 'thanksgiving'.

Evil Things that are not of God.

Faith Belief in God.

Festivals Special times of celebration in the church year, e.g. Easter, Christmas.

Font The piece of 'furniture' that contains water for baptisms, often near the church's main door.

Garden of Eden The area where God placed Adam and Eve.

Gentiles People who are not Jewish; the non-Jewish nations.

Gethsemane The garden where Jesus prayed just before his arrest.

God The supreme being who made the world.

Godparents Sponsors who promise to bring a child up as a Christian at his or her Baptism.

Good Friday The day that Jesus was crucified.

Gospels The books that hold the stories about the life of Jesus: Matthew, Mark, Luke and John.

Grace The loving and undeserved help that God gives to his people.

Heaven The place where God dwells, and where Christians hope to go after death.

Holy Something that is special, concerned with God.

Holy Communion Another name for the Eucharist.

Holy Spirit The third part of the Trinity, that is an aspect of God: Father, Son and Holy Spirit, three parts, but one God. Often seen in windows or artwork as a dove or flames.

Incarnation The birth of Jesus as a man; he was human, but divine.

Jesus Christ The second person of the Trinity, that is an aspect of God: Father, Son and Holy Spirit.

He was born in Bethlehem and lived as a man for about 33 years, before being crucified by the Romans and returning to live with God the Father.

Jews   God's people, called by him to obey the laws given to Moses, and to follow him. Jesus was a Jew.

Joseph   Jesus' earthly father, married to Mary. He was a carpenter.

Kingdom of God God's new Kingdom on earth and in Heaven; a Kingdom of love. Jesus taught the people stories about the Kingdom of God.

Last Supper   The meal that Jesus ate with his disciples the night before he died. During the meal he broke bread and poured wine, and instructed the disciples 'to do this in remembrance of me'. This is what we do each time we celebrate Holy Communion.

Lent   The 40-day penitential season from Ash Wednesday to Easter.

Levite   Jewish descendants of the tribe of Levi, who served in the Temple.

Lord's Prayer   The prayer that Jesus gave to his disciples, which starts 'Our Father in heaven'.

Lord's Supper   Another name for Holy Communion or the Eucharist.

Mary   The mother of Jesus, also called 'the Blessed Virgin Mary' (or BVM). For Roman Catholics, Mary is considered to intercede for Christians with her son, Jesus.

Mass   Another name for Holy Communion, or the Eucharist, or the Lord's Supper. Particularly used by Roman Catholics and high Anglicans.

Messiah   Jesus is the Messiah. The name means 'Saviour' or 'King' or 'Anointed One'.

Miracle	A healing or other event that cannot be explained by any natural means. Jesus carried out many miracles, such as the healing of the man with the withered arm, or the calming of the storm.
Monotheism	Belief in one God. Christians, Jews and Muslims all believe in one God.
Moses	The leader who led the Jews out of slavery in Egypt, to the land that God had promised them in Canaan.
New Testament	The last part of the Bible, specifically concerned with Jesus and the building of the new Church. It contains the Gospels, the Epistles (that is, the letters) and the book of Revelation.
Old Testament	The first part of the Bible; the Hebrew Scriptures.
Palestine	The country where Jesus lived, and part of modern-day Israel.
Palm Sunday	Celebrates the day that Jesus rode into Jerusalem on a donkey; the Sunday before Easter.
Passover	The Jewish festival that celebrates the time when God 'passed over' them and allowed them to escape from the Egyptians.
Paul	Previously called Saul; a Pharisee who initially persecuted the followers of Jesus before becoming a Christian himself. He worked specifically with the Gentiles. Many of the Epistles were written by him.
Pentecost	The Christian festival that celebrates the coming of the power of the Holy Spirit to the disciples. Effectively this is the birth of the Church.
Peter	Jesus gave all authority on earth to Peter. He became the leader of the Church, despite initially rejecting Jesus.

Pharisees	Jewish religious leaders who tried to live by the Law of Moses.
Pope	The leader of the Roman Catholic Church.
Prayer	Speaking and listening to God.
Priest	One of three orders in the Christian Church: deacons, priests and bishops. A priest may celebrate Holy Communion, give blessings and forgive sins.
Promised Land	Canaan, the land that God promised to the Jews.
Protestant	A person or a Church that is no longer a part of the Roman Catholic Church. Members of the Church of England are Protestant.
Protestant Churches	Parts of the Church that broke from the Roman Catholic Church, thus seen as pro-testers. The Church of England is a Protestant Church.
Reformation	The period in our history, in the sixteenth century, when many Christians and denominations split away from the Roman Catholic Church.
Repentance	Being sorry for the sins you have committed.
Resurrection	Jesus rose from the dead on the third day after his death.
Revelation	A message from God.
Roman Catholic Church	The worldwide Church that is headed by the Pope.
Sabbath	The Jewish holy day that starts at sunset on Friday and lasts until sunset on Saturday. Also used of the Christian Sunday.
Sacrament	A sacrament is an outward and visible sign of something that is happening spiritually. Anglicans regard Holy Communion and Baptism as sacraments; other denominations consider there are a number of other sacraments.
Sacred	Something that is holy or set aside for God.

Samaritans	People who lived in Samaria, who established another temple other than that in Jerusalem, and who were disliked by the Jews.
Saviour	Another name for Jesus, because by dying for us he saved us from our sins.
Secular	Anything that is not religious.
Sermon	A talk by an authorized member of the Christian Church, usually given during worship.
Sin	Wrong things that we do, which separate us from God.
Sunday	For Christians this is the first day of the week, and a day of rest.
Temptation	Persuasion to do something that is wrong or sinful.
Ten Commandments	The ten rules given by God to Moses on Mount Sinai.
Theist	Someone who believes that God exists.
Transubstantiation	Belief by Roman Catholics that the bread and the wine actually become the body and blood of Jesus during Holy Communion.
Trinity	One God, but three parts: God as Father, Son and Holy Spirit.
Virgin Birth	The belief that Jesus had no human father, that he was conceived by the power of the Holy Spirit and that Mary was a virgin when she gave birth to him.
Virgin Mary	Another name for Mary, the mother of Jesus.
Worship	A time of praise to God by the congregation, sometimes involving prayer, singing and listening to sermons.
Worshipper	One who worships God.
Yahweh	The Hebrew word for God. Used by the Roman Catholic Church, and sometimes the Anglican Church.

Index

131

Index

Index